Praise for REFINE AND RESTORE

"Rachel Swanson's words will be a breath of fresh air for your faith, a source of hope, and a reminder that even when you can't understand God's plans, you can still trust His heart. When you finish the last page of this book you'll know no matter how it feels right now, your story isn't over yet."

—Holley Gerth, *Wall Street Journal* bestselling author of *What Your Heart Needs for the Hard Days*

"If you've been feeling stagnant, unsure of your purpose, or have the sense God is inviting you to something more, REFINE AND RESTORE will leave you feeling inspired to take a leap of faith with Him into an adventure of a lifetime."

—Rebekah Lyons, author of *You Are Free* and *Freefall to Fly*

"Rachel is a gift to those feeling lost or overwhelmed by the lies they are believing about themselves. REFINE AND RESTORE brings you into Rachel's personal journey of wrestling with these same thoughts and issues, while inviting you into the refining process of stripping away the lies, restoring the truth of your identity, and then arming you with the tools to live out your God-given destiny in Christ."

—Kate Crocco, confidence and mindset coach

"Rachel is a truth teller. In REFINE AND RESTORE, she shares her story with a raw vulnerability, drawing you to see the workings of God behind, in, and through every moment, both in her life and in yours. The call to embrace Jesus and to risk following Him with abandoned trust flows from every page. Read it and you will find your story in her story, but most importantly, you'll find it in His."

—Stasi Eldredge, *New York Times* bestselling coauthor of *Captivating*, director of women's ministries at Ransomed Heart

"At some point, we ask the questions, *Who am I really? Why do I feel distant from God? Is God really who He says He is?* Rachel walks you through her stories of faith as she openly shares about her journey of how she went from seeking the world for significance to experiencing the Christian high, to stagnant faith, to ultimately discovering her true self and the truth about God and revitalizing her faith. Breaking down the true definition of purpose, calling, and understanding our role with God, Rachel compels you to step into the invitation God is beckoning you into with Him and following His lead."

—Alli Worthington, author of *Breaking Busy*, *Fierce Faith*, and *The Year of Living Happy*

"Rachel invites you to consider the questions we all wrestle with about faith, purpose, and failed expectations. REFINE AND RESTORE welcomes the reader into a much-needed conversation about secret battles and burdens, bringing them into the light to find true restoration."

—Erin Weidemann, CEO and co-founder of Truth Becomes Her

"This book shakes you in ways you didn't know you needed. It addresses those feelings that so many of us are scared to face. Yet with grace and gumption, it calls forth the purpose God has put on your life and inspires you to take action. REFINE AND RESTORE will revive you in awe-inspiring ways, and awaken and draw dreams from deep within the well of your heart to release them into the world."

—Kelsey Chapman, author and podcaster

"Rachel Swanson's new book, REFINE AND RESTORE, is filled with deeply personal and relatable stories of mistakes and loss, failure and brokenness, but also testimonies of hope, encouragement, and restoration. Her book is a gift to the discouraged ones, those dealing with defeat and distraction, the ones confused about God's great purpose for their lives. Let Rachel's words invite you into a journey of faith and you will find your own heart revived."

—Kate Battistelli, author of *The God Dare* and *Growing Great Kids*, host of the podcast Mom to Mom

"The book you are holding is a direct result of [Rachel's] radical faith in God's guidance. Raw, relatable, and openhearted, REFINE AND RESTORE will help you answer the questions of purpose, calling, and identity, and compel you to walk an intimate path with God, wherever it may lead you. If you're tired of feeling stagnant in your faith and are ready to come alive with a godly passion and purpose yourself, this book is for you."

—Shannon Ethridge, MA, life coach, speaker, and author

of twenty-two books, including the million-copy bestselling Every Woman's Battle series and *The Sexually Confident Wife*

"Rachel's story to finding spiritual freedom will surprise you. But you'll also relate, no doubt. That's what's beautiful about her story—she found freedom, only to realize God needed to grow her up in other ways. Filled with incredibly practical ways to rediscover the passion of Jesus and find freedom for the ache in your soul . . . this book will leave you feeling like you just gained a friend who gets you."

—Dr. Josh and Christi Straub, authors of *What Am I Feeling* and hosts of In This Together podcast

"Rachel shares her story boldly while never forgetting to make the reader feel like a close friend. With bravery, she has done the work of digging deeper into her faith and we are the beneficiaries of that digging. Get ready to be pushed and prompted to step out further in your purpose while learning to give yourself grace as you grow."

—Hannah Brencher, author of *Come Matter Here*

"Rachel Swanson gets it. She's the type of author who feels like an instant friend. That's because she has lived her message and understands how you feel. If you are ready to refine your heart and revive your purpose, this book is for you."

—Becky Thompson, author of the books *Hope Unfolding*, *Love Unending*, and *Truth Unchanging*

Refine

&

Restore

REVIVE *YOUR HEART,*

RELEASE *YOUR PURPOSE*

RACHEL C. SWANSON

New York   Nashville

Copyright © 2019 by Rachel Swanson
Forward copyright © 2019 by Jennifer Dukes Lee
Cover design credit by Jody Waldrup. Illustration credit filo/Getty Images.
Cover copyright © 2019 by Hachette Book Group, Inc.

Hachette Book Group supports the right to free expression and the value of copyright. The purpose of copyright is to encourage writers and artists to produce the creative works that enrich our culture.

The scanning, uploading, and distribution of this book without permission is a theft of the author's intellectual property. If you would like permission to use material from the book (other than for review purposes), please contact permissions@hbgusa.com. Thank you for your support of the author's rights.

FaithWords
Hachette Book Group
1290 Avenue of the Americas, New York, NY 10104
faithwords.com
twitter.com/faithwords

First Edition: October 2019

FaithWords is a division of Hachette Book Group, Inc. The FaithWords name and logo are trademarks of Hachette Book Group, Inc.

The publisher is not responsible for websites (or their content) that are not owned by the publisher.

The Hachette Speakers Bureau provides a wide range of authors for speaking events. To find out more, go to www.hachettespeakersbureau.com or call (866) 376-6591.

Unless otherwise noted, all Scripture quotations are taken from the Holy Bible, New International Version®, NIV®. Copyright ©1973, 1978, 1984, 2011 by Biblica, Inc.™ Used by permission of Zondervan. All rights reserved worldwide. www.zondervan.com The "NIV" and "New International Version" are trademarks registered in the United States Patent and Trademark Office by Biblica, Inc.™ Scripture quotations marked (AMP) are taken from the Amplified Bible, Copyright © 1954, 1958, 1962, 1964, 1965, 1987 by the Lockman Foundation. Used by permission.
Scripture quotations marked (CEV) are from the Contemporary English Version Copyright © 1991, 1992, 1995 by American Bible Society. Used by Permission.
Scripture quotations marked (CSB) have been taken from the Christian Standard Bible®, Copyright © 2017 by Holman Bible Publishers. Used by permission. Christian Standard Bible® and CSB® are federally registered trademarks of Holman Bible Publishers.
Scripture quotations marked (ESV) are from the ESV® Bible (the Holy Bible, English Standard Version®). ESV® Permanent Text Edition® (2016). Copyright © 2001 by Crossway, a publishing ministry of Good News Publishers. The ESV® text has been reproduced in cooperation with and by permission of Good News Publishers. Unauthorized reproduction of this publication is prohibited. All rights reserved.
Scriptures noted (NASB) are taken from the New American Standard Bible®, copyright © 1960, 1962, 1963, 1968, 1972, 1975, 1977, 1995 by the Lockman Foundation. Used by permission.
Scripture quotations marked (NIrV) are taken from the Holy Bible, New International Reader's Version®, NIrV® Copyright © 1995, 1996, 1998, 2014 by Biblica, Inc.™ Used by permission of Zondervan. All rights reserved worldwide. www.zondervan.com The "NIrV" and "New International Reader's Version" are trademarks registered in the United States Patent and Trademark Office by Biblica, Inc.™
Scripture quotations marked (NKJV) are taken from the New King James Version®. Copyright © 1982 by Thomas Nelson. Used by permission. All rights reserved.
Scripture quotations marked (NLT) are taken from the Holy Bible, New Living Translation, copyright © 1996, 2004, 2007 by Tyndale House Foundation. Used by permission of Tyndale House Publishers, Inc., Carol Stream, Illinois 60188. All rights reserved.
"Oceans (Where My Feet May Fail)" by Joel Houston, Matt Crocker, Salomon Ligthelm © 2013 Hillsong Music Publishing Australia (APRA) (adm. at CapitolCMGPublishing.com). All rights reserved. Used by permission.

Library of Congress Cataloging-in-Publication Data
Names: Swanson, Rachel C., author.
Title: Refine and restore : revive your heart, release your purpose / Rachel C. Swanson.
Description: first [edition]. | New York : Faith Words, 2019. | Includes bibliographical references.
Identifiers: LCCN 2019007477 | ISBN 9781546013440 (trade pbk.) | ISBN 9781546013433 (ebook)
Subjects: LCSH: Christian women--Religious life.
Classification: LCC BV4527 .S875 2019 | DDC 248.8/43--dc23
LC record available at https://lccn.loc.gov/2019007477

ISBNs: 978-1-5460-1344-0 (trade pbk.), 978-1-5460-1343-3 (ebook)

Printed in the United States of America

LSC-C

10 9 8 7 6 5 4 3 2 1

Dedicated to Nicole Edgmond who, with Jesus, helped to refine and restore my heart and soul.

CONTENTS

FOREWORD

As a writer, I have come to believe that one of the most important gifts we can give our readers is this: an honest account of how it all unfolded. Truth-telling is a rare and needed offering in an over-filtered world. We all say we want authenticity, but then we hide the most painful, ugly parts of our lives.

It's always an act of bravery to tell your story. Braver still: to strip away every filter before you start sharing it.

In my own books, when it comes to personal revelation, I've always wanted to figure out where the line of personal comfort is drawn. And then, if I am brave enough, I take a giant leap over it.

I value authenticity, and I know you do too.

Here's the good news: that's what you get in this book. That's what you get in this author. My dear friend Rachel Swanson is inviting you to take a giant leap over your own line of personal comfort, to find Jesus waiting to catch you on the other side.

Know this: your guide is trustworthy. Rachel is a daring, courageous woman with a love for God's Word and for His daughters. She has reached deep inside herself to walk through the process of refinement and restoration.

Her conversion story is nothing short of miraculous, but like most of us, her story doesn't end with her salvation. That was just the beginning.

Oswald Chambers once wrote, "Spiritual maturity is not reached by the passing of the years, but by obedience to the will of God."

Simply put, we don't mature in faith by existing. It takes real work, real focus, real obedience, and as Rachel shows us, real honesty.

In a quick-fix culture, we subscribe to the defective notion that this soul-shaping work ought to come with ease and rapidity. But if you've ever seen an old piece of furniture that has been restored and refined, you know that the process is lengthy. Old paint or varnish is stripped away from the beat-up furniture. Then it is sanded with an abrasive before it can be brought to its polished state of luster—*before it can truly shine*.

Our personal restoration is not so different. For us to truly shine, there are things that God must strip away and sand down. My old friend Pastor Dave used to tell me that sandpaper is, strangely perhaps, the way that the grace of God works sometimes. We want to think that grace is always soft and billowy like cotton. But without the grit of the sandpaper, we'll never truly change. Grace, in this way, can feel uncomfortable and abrasive, but it always produces the desired result of a life restored and refined.

When we rub against "grace like sandpaper," might we be made new too?

Rachel knows this kind of grace. She had to walk a long road through refinement as rough edges were smoothed.

It's her story to tell, but I can promise you that Rachel has arrived at a place where—like an old piece of furniture or an antique tractor—she was restored. And in the midst of this, she has found her calling, not only in women's ministry, but also right in her own home.

What does all of this mean for you?

Rachel is about to lead you on a four-part journey that will revive, refine, restore, and release you. She leaves no stone unturned. Reading this book, you will confront your relationship with finances, friendships, failures, food. You will be challenged to ask yourself hard questions about unhealthy habits, such as gossiping and self-loathing.

Yes, Rachel is inviting you into a journey of *her* heart, but she's also inviting you into a journey of your *own*.

Let "grace like sandpaper" do its work in you.

As Rachel's friend, it's been my joy to watch the incredible and beautiful transformation that has come when Rachel obediently took this journey. There's a boldness to her that I find so refreshing, mostly because I'm someone with a long history of wanting the approval of others. I asked her about that boldness recently. And this is what she told me:

"I am more comfortable in my skin, and I understand my identity even deeper than ever before. I can be vulnerable, because I don't tie my identity to what others think of me. My life is based on my identity in God, and in my relationship with Him. That is why I am able to step out confidently—or even not so confidently—into these unknown places with Him."

But Rachel and I don't want you to settle for just feeling good about yourself. We want you to step out too. We want you to partner with God in ways you never thought possible.

Suit up, new friend. Report for duty. God is calling you to an exciting new way of living.

—Jennifer Dukes Lee
author of *It's All Under Control*

Refine
&
Restore

Section 1

REVIVE

You who have shown me many troubles
and distresses
   Will revive me again,
   And will bring me up again from the
depths of the earth.

Psalm 71:20, NASB

The Not-So-Perfect Christian Life

There's a thought hovering in your mind you don't dare utter out loud, because to utter it would be to claim something's wrong. And nothing is wrong, right? You're fine. I'm fine! We're all just fine.

At least, that's how we pretend to be.

However, the thought nags at you: *Why does this Christian life feel so . . . empty?*

Like many important things begging for your attention, you ignore it. Like an annoying health bill that always pops up again out of nowhere demanding for more money, even though you thought it was fully paid. You continue to ignore it, because really, it's not that urgent, right? There will be a better time to figure it out later and a grace period before it heads to collections. And maybe it will just go away on its own if you ignore the thought long enough.

But instead of fading, the feeling gets stronger. Slowly,

like a thorny vine inside you. A pain-numbing, unsettled feeling that you can't quite place.

It feels silly, though, right? Ignoring this thought seems better, safer. Everyone else seems to be so happy, fulfilled, confident.

I thought this until I began to ask around and discovered there are more of us struggling with this than I once thought. It's time to bring it out into the light.

CHAPTER 1

Lacking Abundance

I needed air.

Feeling suffocated under the weight of my emotions, I coaxed my barely walking seventeen-month-old twin boys out onto our warm patio. The autumn Santa Ana breeze was working its way through the afternoon sky, rustling the fallen leaves. Awkwardly, I tried to find a comfortable sitting position for my much-too-big-for-me belly growing "Wannabe Twin 3," due to make her arrival just before Christmas.

But it was no use. I was still uncomfortable, still unsettled, much like my mind and soul. *What happened to the once-abundant life I experienced with Jesus when I first met Him, the real Him, all those years ago? Why do I feel so distant from Him right now?*

Squeals jolted my attention back to the present. I glanced over at my boys cheerfully prodding a pill bug (or what I call a "roly-poly"), which curled into a ball, trying to protect itself from the tiny but mighty-for-a-pill-bug-sized hands. Unfortunately for our new friend, the term "gentle," although in their vocabulary of understood words, hadn't quite reached through to my twins' nervous systems yet.

Poor roly-poly will probably get stuck staying curled up for a while, if he even survives.

Sometimes, I wish I could curl up into a ball and forget about life for a while.

I sighed, my thoughts trailing yet again from one moment wishing for a more fulfilling life to the next feeling utterly guilty for even thinking such a thought. I had so much. More than I deserved. I was grateful. But true contentment felt out of my reach.

I still felt like something was missing.

Church these days felt more like a country club where I must dress to impress, instead of meeting with the bled and broken-for-us Jesus. Passion and zest for my job as a dental hygienist was waning, even though I excelled in it and loved many aspects of it. *Perhaps I should go into ministry to experience more of Him?* Motherhood—although expected to be hard, especially my first experience with not one, but two babies at the same time—left me wondering more and more every day, *Who is this Rachel girl? Is she still even here under the piles of diapers and bottles?* Joy—definitely lacking. And don't tell me I need more faith like many well-meaning Christians say; I still had faith.

I remembered back to when Jesus felt so vividly present when I first became a believer eleven years earlier, in October 2002. How intimately He met me when I said that first soul-changing prayer to Him. How He showed up that night in supernatural ways most people have a hard time believing—which is silly, because isn't God supernatural? And yet, somewhere along the way, I think I stopped believing in the supernatural power of our Creator too.

I had the spiritual high everyone talks about when they first become a "Christian" or "accept Jesus into their heart." I experienced the radical change from Mormon to Christian—or as I like to define it: having a personal relationship with Jesus. The total void I'd felt my entire life up to this point was finally filled with a fullness I lack enough words to describe. But I'll try. Think of a massive ocean wave drenching you on a blistering hot day, compelling you from shore to dive straight in as you fully immerse yourself in the refreshing swirl of intoxicating blue. This is what Jesus does to you when He gets into you.

God was near and dear to me then. He was alive and very much active. The aching void was gone. He was real and present. Why can't I say that with confidence now? What changed?

A few years into my walk and journey with God, I began to think God had forgotten all about me. I questioned whether or not I was "saved." Perhaps I had too much junk from my past preventing full restoration. Perhaps His grace wasn't as sufficient for me as it was for everyone else. Perhaps being "good enough" isn't good enough to have the fully vibrant relationship I deeply wanted to experience with Jesus.

Maybe I'm not experiencing the fullness of what can be experienced in life with God because I'm missing something vitally important. But what? Really, I have everything.

In the practical sense, it wasn't like I was going through any major life crisis. Things were fairly stable. We had enough money to pay our bills and have a little fun too. Our church community was strong. I loved my career as a dental hygienist, especially the flexibility it gave me to be a mom and nurture my family. Things were...good!

Here's the kicker: I loved Jesus. At least I thought I did. I mean, I read my Bible...okay, *tried* to read my Bible. Maybe I wasn't feeling so motivated in this season to read it, as sleep always seemed to be a priority, especially as a mom of twins and then being hugely pregnant again. When I did read the Word, it felt dry. So why try?

I started to think maybe I could try praying in this season. So I tried. Honestly, some days I really did try. But most days no words would come. Anytime I tried, it felt like a hard, bitter ball rammed down my throat with painful emotions threatening to exude past my "I'm fine" control point. Or I felt so empty of emotion that I was merely chanting empty words.

I kept up the charade of the masked Christian life I was supposed to play out. I kept pretending life was great because, to the external eye, it was! I had everything. And really, if life was falling apart externally, would things be different internally than they currently felt?

I've encountered hundreds of people who have next to nothing, and yet their faith sustains them. Shoot, not only does it sustain them, but they are also thriving with confidence, fully content, and are some of the most joyful people I've ever met.

No matter how much I struggled, questioning my faith altogether was, quite frankly, out of the question. I knew neither going back to my Mormon roots nor running away from God altogether (as I had done in my teenage years) was a good option. God had miraculously met me those many years ago. This unforgettable memory reminds me of the truth when my trust begins to falter. The old has gone, the new has come (2 Cor. 5:17). I'm not who I was. I'm not filled to the deepest depths of empty like I was before. And I'm never going back to that previous state.

So why now, eleven years later in my journey with the Abundant Life Giver, does the Christian life seem to lack its luster? Where did I go wrong?

Maybe we all need to go back two thousand years and live in the actual presence of Jesus—performing miracles, raising the dead, turning water to wine, and healing the sick with one touch of His robe—to remember the depth of His life-giving presence. Right now, I could use a touch of that robe.

Lord, is this the way the Christian life is supposed to be? So fake, so dull, so boring, so... lifeless? I thought you were, and are, *the Abundant Life Giver?*

If you're anything like me, this is what you've been too scared to utter out loud. Because everyone knows Jesus means life. And to say the truth of what you're feeling—that living a Christian life lacks meaning—is to say that a life with Jesus is dull and boring. But that's just wrong. Right?

It has to be wrong. Jesus even said Himself, "I came that [you] may have life and have it abundantly" (John 10:10).

Sure, the verse is talking in part about experiencing the gift of salvation—a fancy name for life in heaven to those who believe in Him. This *is* an abundant gift. I want this. I need this. I mean, who doesn't?

But, friend, aren't we still missing something? What about experiencing an abundant life now? Is this possible? And if so, how? The cliché answer is: Jesus.

It's always Jesus, right?

Okay, but I do have faith in Jesus and believe in Him. Why then do I feel so disillusioned with this so-called abundant Christian life?

Suddenly, I noticed the roly-poly making his break back to the dirt. He survived! A few feet away, my twins found another friend to interrogate—Mr. Grasshopper.

Hmm, perhaps I will make it too?

I hobbled over to get closer to my twins (and got ready to teach them again about the word "gentle"), when I felt their baby sister in my belly prodding me with her elbow. It was almost as if God was elbowing me too, trying to nudge me into believing in His pursuit of me, regardless of how I felt.

Then another unuttered question began to simmer: *Perhaps this Abundant Life Giver isn't really all He's cracked up to be?*

BREAKING POINT

"Don't be mad at me . . . ," he said.

I collapsed into tears. I mean, I was definitely hormonal—pregnancy will do that to you. But it was so much more than that.

Tears of *Oh crap, I really do need this right now* fell as I realized my husband had signed me up for a four-day women's retreat without consulting me first. I tried to wrap my mind around being forced to leave with two babies in diapers toddling around and a complicated pregnancy.

My husband consoled me as I tried to dry sobbing tears that just wouldn't stop. The sobs didn't come from a place of hurt but from a place of acknowledgment. Someone else was validating the pain they saw me living in and the embarrassment of knowing I needed help.

He was right. I would have never signed up on my own. Not in the current state I was in, even though I knew I needed this. Thankfully (for his sake), I was more shocked than mad at him for doing it.

I wouldn't know a single person at this retreat; ironically, that was the good part. Less pressure to mingle and expose this less than sightly side of myself I'd been fighting so hard to keep hidden. Fewer moments of uncontrollable, exploding emotions in front of others, especially since I didn't understand these emotions myself.

Even though I appreciated Jeff acknowledging my stagnant heart, I *was* mad—just not at him. I was mad to be in this position where I needed help. Mad to be feeling so lost, so void, so lifeless, when I knew my heart should feel so full.

Mad at God for quenching me of His abundant love, putting me in this situation.

It was Him, not me. His fault, not mine. My stagnant state was due to Him leaving me high and dry. At least that's what I wanted to believe.

I felt empty of His love, but I knew deep down in my bones I wasn't truly as far away from Him as I felt. He was still there, the Life Giver was still there, somewhere, perhaps sustaining me in ways I will never know in this life.

But here's the thing I've come to realize now: emotions, while healthy to acknowledge, aren't always derived from truth.

While my heart felt empty, my head knew I wasn't completely void of His love. While my heart felt angry, my head knew I was running from the True Intimacy that could be had. While my heart felt confused, my head knew where I could go to find Truth.

You know what I'm talking about, right? Maybe you're already feeling uncomfortable with this acknowledgment that something inside of you is off. But this is where we have to start: by getting honest with ourselves and facing those hard, refining questions. I want you to go from stagnant faith to walking on water with Jesus. To follow Him on an exhilarating ride and journey to places you never even dreamed of walking with Him. To go from barely surviving to thriving. Living in ways God has clearly spelled out for us to live by through His Bible. Obeying Jesus, not out of duty but out of love for Him, and experiencing the fullness of life in the process.

The reason you need to take this step is because I believe your heart is yearning for this kind of revival. To revive your heart, we need to refine and restore your soul to what is true.

Trust me as someone who has lived through it and survived to tell you how.

You need to ask yourself honestly, "Am I ready to go through the soul work to experience the abundant life?" I hope the answer is yes.

The way I see it, you have two options. You can either close this book and continue living a lackluster life with a sense of emptiness. Or you can keep reading to discover, as I did, what went missing in the equation and begin to experience the full, exhilarating, abundant life you and I are meant live right now.

I hope you will decide the latter, because your soul and lifelong joy depend on it.

A DIVINE ENCOUNTER

I had no choice but to face the truth of my emotions with the One who held me captive that day. I had no cell phone service at the women's retreat, so texting a friend was out. Numbing myself with Facebook was definitely out. So there I sat, by myself, on the upstairs patio of a quaint little barn-house looking over the vast green grass, honey-colored fields, and the multitude of roses blooming down below. All the women were scattered around the property, connecting with Jesus in their thoughts and prayers.

Why does this have to be so hard? I sighed and sat back in the rocking chair, rubbing my belly, trying to calm my daughter's flipping motions. Or perhaps it was my own stomach flipping and turning in knots as I thought about this forced time to connect with Jesus when it had been too long. Or maybe I was having contractions!

Calm down, Rachel. Stop overreacting.

But the nerves were there. An anticipation for something...I didn't even know what exactly. Perhaps the fear of what I would face during this time alone. Well, not quite alone...

I reached for my Bible and attempted to open it. Stopping short, I pulled back and decided just talking it out with Him would probably be better. Less Bible stuff to fill my mind and think about because that could be too distracting, right?

Gazing out at the horizon with the sun directly over me but the patio awning protecting me, I felt the honest questions start to trickle forth with sudden clarity:

Why, God, do I feel so empty when my life is so full?
Why does this Christian walk have to be so dang hard?
Why don't we have a relationship anymore like we used to?
What is Your purpose for me?

I felt the burn of emotions rising. I listened, but no answers came. Stinging tears of frustration pierced my eyes as I felt alone once again. Honestly, I didn't need any of His Christian responses to my questions anyway.

Before too long, I found myself sobbing and screaming (as mutedly as I could so no one would hear me), "All of this is Your fault, God! Why don't You answer me? Do You even love me? Who am I, really? Who *are* You? Please just take all these dark and depressed thoughts and emotions away from me!"

I kept unloading the weight of my burdens, everything I was holding on to. All the hardships I was facing in motherhood and with my difficult pregnancy. All the fears I had about quitting my job and the career I had worked so hard for to stay home with my babies. The desire for deeper intimacy with my husband. The string of rejections from so-called friends over the years. The black-sheep status I had in my family because I turned my back on their faith, the faith I was raised to believe. Fears, failures, faults—all on the table for Him to see how bad life was...how bad I *really* was.

After what felt like hours of unleashing my wrath, confusion, sorrow, and anger against God, I was sure He would never speak to me again.

What happened next nearly knocked me flat. I felt...

Nearness.

His nearness.

Loving nearness...toward me.

An undeniable holy presence.

Broken and trembling, I felt the warmth of His invisible arms enfolding me. Wrapping around me. And this broke me even more...but in a beautiful way.

Through this unveiled brokenness, light was beginning to shine through the cracks of my soul. Healing Light. Life-giving Light. The Light I'd been longing to feel again for far too long.

Peace entered next. A healing peace. A surrendered peace as I gave Him the rightful throne over my heart, head, and mind once again.

The bell gonged, signaling the next session. Disoriented and a bit confused about what had just happened, I wiped my tears and took a deep breath. Walking down the stairs, across the lawn to the next session, I knew this was the beginning of something new once again.

Borrow This Reviving Prayer When Words Are Few

Dear Father in heaven, give me the courage to openly and honestly share with You my heart— where I'm struggling, what I'm questioning, how I'm wrestling with my emotions. I know this is the start to deeper intimacy with You when I share my whole heart, and I know I will receive Your grace and love even though I'm scared to open up with You. I'm ready to receive whatever You will have me receive and believe in the truth of who You really are once again. In Jesus's name, amen.

CHAPTER 2

Truth Revealed

He told me after a week of dating, on the night of our first kiss, that we were going to get married. This didn't completely shock me. Mormon boys tend to go hard and fast, not in the worldly way, but in the let's-get-married-so-we-can-start-having-babies way. I'm not sure why this is, but I have my assumptions.

He stroked my straightened hair as I looked into his hopeful eyes. Such innocence lived there. Innocence I was lacking.

You see, he didn't know the real me. He knew only that I was from a strong Mormon background with a lifetime of Mormon roots. And apparently, he had had some sort of dream that told him he would marry a girl named Rachel. But the real me, hiding behind the veil of outward appearances and Mormon pretenses, was a girl who was very broken and torn by her current beliefs.

He didn't know about the multiple men and sinful

relationships of my past. He didn't know about my party-girl drinking episodes over the past freshman year of college. He didn't know the wrestling going on in my mind because I'd recently hit rock bottom and was finally searching for truth about this whole God and religion business.

And I didn't know how to tell him, for fear of losing something good. I didn't want to ruin this chance of love with a guy whom I had idolized in high school. He was the homecoming king my sophomore year—his senior year—and although we had known each other during that time, sparks weren't officially flying yet. There were perhaps a few moments I had noticed our mutual affection.

But it wasn't until now, after recently coming back from his two-year stint as a missionary (normal and expected for Mormon boys), that a noticeable interest was formed—rather quickly. He was tall, dark (tan), and handsome. Popular. Great family. Liked by every girl. He was wicked smart and would likely have a distinguished career in the future. My family more than approved of him and approved of us dating (especially due to my not-so-great recent relationships). And here he was saying he was going to marry me…

It was every girl's dream.

Any Mormon girl in their right mind would say yes… and, yet, I honestly didn't know what to say.

The problem was that I was heavily debating this whole religion thing. Especially Mormonism. And the more I researched it, the more and more I wrestled with the question of "Why isn't this all lining up?"

At this point, I would have called myself agnostic. I believed there was a God or higher being but wasn't sure about this whole Jesus figure and the Bible. Anytime I pictured God I always had a sense He was disappointed in me and that I would never measure up to His standards. I would never make it to the celestial Kingdom that all Mormons strive for.

But living my life the way I wanted wasn't fulfilling either. In fact, it was leaving a giant, gaping hole of hollowness and emptiness, destroying my soul.

No amount of attention, love, alcohol, food (or lack thereof), shopping, or popularity was filling that depth. It was fathomless. Which is why I started to believe, "There's got to be more to life than this..."

* * *

I had the most boring job that summer, but it was that job that enabled me to find truth.

I worked at a booth on the marina ten minutes from my parents' house, accepting tickets from people taking their boats down to the dock of giant Lake Oroville. It's the same lake I enjoyed boating, wakeboarding, and fishing on with my family when I was younger. I still remember the one island we would boat to, to eat our lunch: tuna fish sandwiches, nacho cheese Doritos (because those are the best), and bags of watermelon slices. My feet would get sucked into the muddy shore as I gazed above at the mile-high pine trees surrounding me within the steep canyon walls racing to the water's edge.

Initially, I was excited to be working at the lake I grew up at, awash with so many fond memories. But as I took money from customers, giving them tickets to enter and watching them go have a blast, sitting by myself for the next six to eight hours with only old VCR movies to watch (no internet) brought a wave of boredom.

It was 2002, so this was pre–social media craze. I bought my first cell phone eight months prior, which was just a flip phone you get for free these days. So I would check out the old VCR movies from the marina and watch them during work hours to pass the time. But soon those old movies got, well, old. And the growing ache to understand the rooted truths of the Bible gnawed at me to the point that I decided to start the process of deeper discovery.

So in June 2002 I took my giant Mormon Bible—a compilation of other books Mormons believe, making it twice the size of the Bible—and started reading through the first book, Genesis. The first few chapters weren't anything new. I already knew how the Bible explained the creation of the world and the first people of this earth, Adam and Eve. I knew about Noah and the ark, the flood and how the animals came in pairs to board the ship. I'd heard about Cain and Abel but didn't really know the full context of that story until I read through it. As I read on, I became more aware of how much I didn't know or hadn't really read on my own before.

When I flipped over to the New Testament, which starts with Matthew, another familiar story popped into view— the story of Jesus's birth. Again, this was familiar, because the Christmas story of Jesus's birth is told in so many ways in our culture. But when I came to Jesus the adult, and read through the stories telling of the miracles he performed, his teachings, and even parts of his death and resurrection, it all came alive and touched me in ways I hadn't felt before. I read through most of Matthew, but eventually found myself in James and Philippians, which is where my wheels really started to turn.

In these books of the Bible, it says that by faith you are saved, not by actions or good deeds (James 2:14–20, Phil. 3:9). This was different from what I was raised to believe. I still remember attending early-morning Mormon classes before school and one lesson in particular giving me a hopeless feeling about God. The teacher proceeded to draw a diagram of a ladder on the whiteboard with certain elements between each rung that were required for us to reach the highest Kingdom of heaven (again, another aspect of Mormon theology). He put in baptism, temple endowments, and a host of other elements that created a works-based theology. The teacher talked about how tithing, being "clean" (meaning no lying, cursing, drinking caffeine, etc.), and a temple marriage were all required. This teaching made me see God as someone who was a high and mighty being waiting for me to mess up so that He could crush me and punish me for not doing the right things.

But that summer, I continued to read in the Bible about a God who is loving, kind, gentle, and compassionate toward those who love Him. He is full of grace and sees our iniquities "as white as snow" (Isaiah 1:8). I continued to pore through Scripture, reading passages that connected God, Jesus, and the Holy Spirit as one, not as three separate beings. I couldn't find anything that had to do with the three Kingdoms of heaven, in which the Mormon faith believed. The only passage I could find was one that states, "There are also celestial bodies and terrestrial bodies; but the glory of the celestial is one, and the glory of the terrestrial is another. There is one glory of the sun, another glory of the moon, and another glory of the stars; for one star differs from another star in glory" (1 Cor. 15:40–41, NKJV). Other translations say, "There are also heavenly bodies and there are earthly bodies; but the splendor of the heavenly bodies is one kind, and the splendor of the earthly bodies is another" (1 Cor. 15:40–41). Paul, the author of First Corinthians, is explaining how we have a body here on earth, but we hold a spirit body as well. Each one holds its own importance. This says nothing about heaven being split into three heavens—celestial, telestial, and terrestrial—as Mormons believe. And if that was such a key piece of understanding, don't you think it would be cited multiple times in Scripture?

God tends to repeat key truths in the Bible to illustrate levels of importance in what He wants us to learn and understand. There are some things that are talked about sparingly, and we do our best to understand what God means by them. But as a whole, God is not trying to make this understanding of faith difficult for us. He is truly keeping it simple; yet it's harder to apply the truths to our heart, mind, and soul.

When I was home that summer working in that little marina booth, I continued searching for more answers to my questions about God. I would take what I read in the Bible in that booth and search for more information online. Again, this was 2002, when the available material about religions and faith wasn't anything like it is today. I actually had a hard time finding information from others who had left the Mormon Church or Biblical citations that backed up their teaching (that's not an issue today). Much of what I read referred to the Book of Mormon, Doctrine and Covenants, or the Pearl of Great Price, additional books that were added to the Bible, written by Joseph Smith in the 1800s, when this religion was born. I read articles from prophets who claimed new theology had been revealed to them and they would add this to their teaching.

But I wanted to know where this was in the Bible—a sound work of words more than two thousand years old, which has stood the test of time. It's backed by multiple scholars, historians, and theologians attesting to the truth and accuracy of what is now bound as the Holy Book—still the number one book sold in the world. Researching other religions and their books, their accuracy and theology, just didn't compare to the scientific accuracy of the actual Bible. Therefore, I quickly realized there had to be something to this whole Christianity thing in relation to this ancient text.

Months went by as I researched, read, and relentlessly pursued truth. My brain became more and more rattled with this new way of thinking. I could feel the foundation my entire life had been built on—all of the "truths" my parents had poured into me—breaking up underneath me.

Inevitably, summer came to an end, and back to college I went for my sophomore year. I continued my questions with a few of my close Christian friends. One in particular—Karen, my best friend, whom I met in the dorms—became a key friendship, which eventually ignited my faith.

We lived in a small house near campus, cheap rent and perfect for the simple college-life atmosphere. Fond memories well up in me of multiple evenings when I would knock on the door to her room and ask if we could chat about God. I always sensed her hesitancy, because she used to be a different faith as well, and she was still working through changes of her own about her belief in God. However, I thought it was perfect as we wrestled together. She pointed out various key points through what she was learning at the Bible study she attended.

One day, I found myself on campus at the U—a big open plaza area on the Cal Poly (California Polytechnic), San Luis Obispo, campus—sitting at an outdoor table where people congregated or were walking to class. We were with Karen's Bible study leader and had an hour break before our next class. I used the next hour asking her leader a few questions I was confused by within the Christian faith. "Tell me about this grace part of what you believe. So there's no list of things you must do to get to heaven? You don't have to be baptized, tithe, go to the temple, and do all these things to achieve God's favor to enter heaven someday?"

Her name was Amy. She had the brightest smile and one of the most tender hearts toward God I've ever known. And her deep understanding of the Bible didn't go unnoticed either.

"Have you read the book of James yet?" she replied.

"Sort of." *Wasn't that the one about faith and not works?*

She grinned. "Well, let's look at it now."

Opening her Bible without even a hint of timidity (whereas I felt uncomfortable sitting in public where my non-Christian friends—like my sorority sisters—might see me), she went straight to the chapter. Truth be told, opening the Bible in public didn't feel cool. It could ruin my popularity streak. But my persistence to find truth defeated my trepidation.

"Let's read this together..." She scooted over to me so that I could read it with her. She read James 2:14–26 out loud, then asked me what I thought it was saying.

"Well..." I hated pop quizzes. "It sounds like it says that works—like baptism, tithing, etc.—aren't what saves you. It's by faith. Although I'm confused. Don't you need works and faith together? It seems like this is still somewhat important."

"Yes, works are still important. But this is from the outflow of your faith and belief in Jesus. If you believe in Jesus, Who saves us from eternal death and separation from God, receiving the gift of the Holy Spirit in your life through your belief in Him, then you will enter God's Kingdom after you die. You also experience His presence in your life now, which will bring peace, joy, and purpose to your steps regardless of what you face. There's a fullness in your heart that's hard to describe. But through faith in Him, this *fullness* enters in, and our actions will then precede our faith. Does this make sense?"

To be honest, it was a lot to digest and took more years from that moment on to understand what she had shared. But what I gained in that conversation was enough for me to begin feeling the weight of a works-based theology fall off my shoulders.

I didn't have to be perfect to be accepted by God.

I didn't have to do all the things I felt like I needed to do in order to experience God's love in my life.

I didn't have to do anything but love and accept Jesus into my heart to receive the love and grace He freely extends back to me.

In fact, He already extends that love and grace freely, but it's up to me to receive it and believe it's true.

I still wasn't ready to make any life-changing decisions in this public place where others might see me. But it did initiate the next step: attending the Campus Crusade for Christ fall retreat the following month.

* * *

People raised their hands in the air, dancing to the beat of the music being played onstage, music that worked in step with words full of holy passion. However, I still felt uncomfortable. In the church where I was raised, I was used to sitting in reverence while the organist played quiet hymns.

We never raised our hands or danced to the beat of what was playing. I never experienced joy or real worship.

And yet, the joy here at the Campus Crusade retreat was palpable.

Could I really dance and sing to Jesus in a way that was holy and honors Him? The Bible talks about praising God through dancing and singing to Him. "Let them praise His name with dancing; Let them sing praises to Him," the Psalms declare (Psalm 149:3, NASB). It was all new to me, and I loved it. My heart was infatuated with this way of expressing praise and worship to God.

The beat infiltrated my ears as my heart leaped spontaneously. Silent tears crept from my eyes down my cheeks. I wiped them away in the dark room before anyone could see me. However, glancing around me, I noticed I wasn't the only one being affected in this way.

As the weekend retreat went on, I found myself in a small group where we discussed what we were learning about God, and we shared our personal stories. Honestly, I don't remember much about those small groups, but I do remember feeling moved by every message the pastor preached onstage. It was like everything he was sharing was finally making sense to me. All the Bible reading I'd been doing over the past several months—dissecting religions, detangling the truth from the lies—was finally coming to a head. It was all clicking. One piece after the other. Like a puzzle where all the pieces are finally forming into a complete image. I was thrilled, and also terrified, by my predicament.

My heart ached to say yes at the altar call. But I couldn't...

My family would disown me.

My sorority girls would reject me.

My life was a messy reality.

I was broken beyond repair and knew I needed this. In fact, deep down I wanted this.

But what if this isn't really true?

Heading home that evening, I knew I had to decide. I was on the fence of faith. No longer could I deny God. No longer could I deny the truth about Jesus.

But...which faith was the *real* truth?

I was drawn to the message of how it's about a relationship, not about religion. That religion is man-made but a personal relationship with God—through Jesus, who is God in human form, perfect and blameless, sacrificing Himself for us, who paid the penalty of our sins—was compelling and hard to believe at the same time. It's like being sentenced to life in prison, but one day you get the message that someone else took your place to set you free. They paid the debt you owed, even though you deserved it.

Because the truth is none of us deserve this gift. You and I are a hot mess most of the time. We lie to our kids. We covet stuff. We gossip with our friends. We often idolize and worship other things more than God. We may be secretly fantasizing about another man (or woman, for that matter) in lustful ways that are inappropriate at best. We curse too much, drink too much, and pretend like it's all just fine. But we're not. You know it. I know it. Which is why we need someone to save us from ourselves.

I need Jesus. You need Jesus. He is the missing piece in this longing for something more.

Arriving home, I locked myself in my bedroom. I needed to be alone, in the dark. I was ready to know without a doubt the truth of all this faith business once and for all.

I was wracked with emotions: fear, confusion, sorrow, and exhaustion piled on top of me. Mostly the fear element—fear of getting this wrong, fear of what others would think if I decided to pursue this faith, fear of rejection by my family and current non-Christian friends.

But a deeper fear lay restless in my soul: fear of living my life any longer feeling void of God's love.

I lay on top of my cheetah-print bedspread, exhausted by the weekend. Staring at the ceiling, I imagined the likely scenarios before me if I decided on this path. I closed my eyes and prayed harder than I've ever prayed in my life. Hours went by, my thoughts vacillating from determined belief to defiant rejection of what I knew in my heart to be true.

There was no going back at this point. I couldn't revert to the life I was living—so worldly, void of purpose and contentment. A bleeding, broken heart had resulted in my rebellion. I had done enough damage, especially through the string of unhealthy relationships I had given way too much of myself for.

I couldn't deny the realness of God anymore. But I was still processing this new image of Jesus and the truth about Him, this Jesus figure who performed miracles and taught about mind-boggling grace, unconditional love, and undeserving forgiveness. He showed up to five thousand people after he was resurrected—which is a fancy way of saying "brought back to life"—demonstrating the ability for us to have life after death if we believe in Him. He was ready to take the weight of all my mistakes if I simply believed and trusted in Him. This is the simplicity of the gospel.

Why is this decision so hard for me to make? I lay there, wondering.

I wanted to know without a shadow of a doubt whether or not the Christian way of living was true. Or was the Mormon way of believing really the truth? There was truth on both sides. I could see that now. But which was right?

After what felt like hours of praying and lots of tears, I knelt on the hardwood floor in a fetal position, crying out these words: "God, I need You. I need to know the truth. I need You to show up powerfully for me, so I can know without a doubt which faith is true. I need to know the truth about who You are . . ."

My muscles ached with tension, my eyes burned from the overwhelming pressure of tears that just wouldn't stop. I was tired but motivated to keep pressing into this until I had a clear answer from Him.

After more praying, I finally spoke with the determination of a racehorse but also in holy submission, knowing Who I was speaking to. "God—" I wrestled with what I was about to say. "Is the Mormon faith, their prophet and leader that started it all—Joseph Smith—and all the teachings of the Mormon faith, true?"

What happened is surreal at best. Instantly the room

grew cold. I felt a dark, oppressive weight on me and shivered with chills all over my body. I heard a resounding "*NO!*" in my mind that felt unearthly and omniscient— God Himself speaking to me. There was a knowing in my soul that it was Him, and it was unlike anything else I've ever experienced.

Overwhelmed by this answer, almost paralyzed with fear, I finally asked the other pressing question rattling my mind: "God, is this Christian faith, or more specifically having a personal relationship with You and all the words of the Bible about Jesus, true?"

Quickly the weight lifted. An indescribable peace fell on top of me, filling me with a joy that is literally indescribable. My eyes were closed, but I promise you I saw through my eyelids white light shining just beyond them. But I was too terrified to open them. I heard a resounding "*YES!*" and could almost feel the embrace of God's arms around me there in that dark room.

I knew the truth. I knew without a shadow of a doubt. I received Jesus into my heart and never looked back.

Let me address the question you might be asking after reading my story: I don't know why some people experience tangible and miraculous evidence of God and others don't. Some people are miraculously healed while others are not. Some experience supernatural manifestations of His presence while others are left trusting in the truth of God's Word without outward expressions of His presence.

But I do know God is real, active, and supernatural in nature.

You may have a tough time believing my story. I've often hid this story from others because it's one of those experiences that defies logic, science, and is definitely supernatural. It's also personal and cannot be confirmed. But I experienced it. Felt it. Believe it. And to the best of my ability, I'm telling you all of it because perhaps you can borrow my testimony if you're still wrestling with this truth-about-God talk as well.

The question I want to nudge you with is this: if you do believe in a supernatural God, why is it so hard to believe in His power to do supernatural things? Many of us don't question the supernatural stories of the Bible. We believe them to be true, and yet those stories seem ancient, right? Therefore, those types of supernatural events don't happen anymore, right?

Or do they?

I've often wondered why God showed up for me the way He did when others may never experience God in this way. The only thing I can conclude is that God knew I would need something tangible to hold on to because the next several years of my life would be a wild roller coaster of difficulty as I clung to this newfound faith I believed in. It would be an easier choice to go back to my Mormon up-bringing, because my family would be happier, I would be able to marry that nice Mormon boy who was infatuated with me, and it would still be a healthier alternative than the current life I was living.

But still, I would have forever felt that void and separation from a true, intimate relationship with God.

* * *

The next few years were anything but easy. As I tried to change my lifestyle from the unhealthy patterns I had been living, certain friends grew distant. Being in the sorority was difficult because I was surrounded by things that didn't help me cultivate a Christian lifestyle. I didn't have the external willpower to control my drinking, which led me to wake up to the worst outcomes. I would say, "Okay, just two drinks," and then find myself passed out drunk in my bed again the next morning with a horrible hangover, unable to remember the events of the night. It's like inviting a recovering alcoholic to a bar—it never ends well.

So I started to get more involved with the campus Christian ministry called Campus Crusade for Christ (now called CRU). I developed new friends who shared similar values about what I was trying to cultivate in my life. As I worked to connect with these Christian girls, I still always felt like an outsider due to my history and the stories of being the classic sorority girl.

Karen was the only Christian friend who seemed to understand me, looking past my past, loving me through my mistakes as I kept messing up here and there.

One day my parents started prodding me: "So, are you going to church?"

"Yes." I hesitated to share more with them. "I started going to this Christian church in the area and I really like it," I finally said.

There was a pause. "Oh!" Then another pause from my mom, before she said, "Well, I'm glad you're exploring a bit...but I encourage you to attend the Mormon church too. I hear there's a good one in that area!"

Really, at this time, they were simply happy I was pursuing church again, since it was no secret to them that I had been pursuing a damaging, unhealthy lifestyle. But as time went on, they continued to ask me, "So, have you checked out the Mormon church yet?"

"Well, no." I couldn't tell them I never planned on going back. Not yet.

"Okay, well, when we visit, we would like to go to that one with you."

Only when my parents visited did I go, out of respect for them.

But I knew I wouldn't be going back to that faith. I knew the truth. A soul-ripping fire ignited my soul as I finally understood why many believers are compelled to raise their hands in worship to Him. My heart grew wild with excitement for Jesus, and I too finally gained the courage one day to raise my palms and sway to the percussion, allowing the truthful words to captivate my soul, while I sang in honor of Him. I didn't care anymore. Unafraid of this beautiful expression of love and devotion toward Him, I praised Him like I was the only one in the room adoring this God I loved with my whole being.

Borrow This Restoring Prayer When Words Are Few

LORD, I'm ready to believe in Your supernatural ability to speak to my heart, mind, and soul. I'm ready for Your truths to be revealed and ask for courage to take the next step with You when so much fear seeks to hold me back. I want to believe. LORD, help me with my unbelief. Draw me nearer to Your Word—the Bible—a living, vivid reminder of who You really are. Give me eyes to see and ears to hear what it is You want me to know and experience with You. I'm ready to love You wholeheartedly. In Jesus's name, amen.

CHAPTER 3

Spiritual High to Stagnant Waters

I would have walked through fire if God told me to. This was the state of my faith for the next several years after I was "saved."

This fire led me to attend a Summer Project—a Christian summer retreat through CRU. I was placed at the South Lake Tahoe location, where I was surrounded by evergreen pines and emerald-blue waters. I bunked in the smallest one-bedroom cabin I've ever seen in my life. Sharing it with two other roommates, even by freshman dorm standards it was tight. The old cabin's wood floors were splintered and worn and collected piles of pebbles and dust from living the camp life. With no dresser or closet to put my clothes into, I lived out of a suitcase for three months.

And yet, it became home to some of my fondest memories. It's where I learned about serving God whole-heartedly despite my circumstances. It's where I grew in my understanding of the Bible. It's where I saw glimpses of my calling to mentor women. It's where I built on my limited understanding of the Bible as I pored through Scripture and enjoyed my discipleship time with other women. I discovered long-lasting friendships—Kate, Kim, and Kristin—yes, my name was the odd one out. We're still friends fourteen years later.

We were all required to get jobs for the summer. This enabled us to positively impact the community through our faith at work. Fortunately, I became one of the assistant managers at Round Table Pizza (a prime summer job for the area), but unfortunately the free pizza every day made me go in search of new clothes by the end of summer.

Small-group time helped me cultivate deeper under-standing of God and stoked the fire in me as I sensed His Spirit at work in my life. I grew radically, soaking it all in, almost like being intoxicated with the fervor of God. I didn't crave what I used to crave anymore. I wasn't seeking the approval of men. I was fueled by a different passion and desire, full of excitement and purpose.

The following summer, after graduating from college with my bachelor's degree, I found myself serving again, this time at Hume Lake Christian Camps. My position there enabled me to float around, filling in different positional needs each week. However, most of the time I filled in gaps for churches or organizations as a camp counselor for girls attending that week. Depending on the week, I would find myself at Wagon Train (fifth and sixth graders), Meadow Ranch (seventh and eighth graders), or

Ponderosa (high schoolers), where my job was to continue spiritual discussion and, of course, keep the girls out of mischief. Trust me, Christian girls can be just as mischievous (and naughty) as non-Christian girls.

These weeks were emotionally and physically exhausting. There were only short breaks on Saturdays after the buses left to take the Jesus-filled campers back home; early dawn the next day would bring in a squirrely group of new, fresh campers as it started all over again.

This was one of the starting points for me in understanding a unique part of my character. In fact, I don't even think I realized it until now: how much I was created for this role—stewarding the hearts of women and teaching them to love God and see His love for them.

Do you know the role or roles you've been created to fulfill? Are you pursuing work that is related to the unique characteristics purposely placed in you by God? This isn't always easy to see. In fact, it often takes a lot of soul searching and intentional redirecting to get us to a place where we are fulfilling our unique purpose in the ways God has called us to play them out.

And sometimes, being the hands and feet of Jesus in ways He asks us to serve isn't glorious or exciting.

On one particular week, I found myself in the camp kitchen, scrubbing thousands of dishes, cups, and pots and pans from the pounds of food campers were eating each week. My hands had never been so chapped. I gained a greater appreciation and respect for the kitchen staff who were assigned that role the entire summer. While scrubbing pots, they would sing worship songs together to pass the time or make up games to keep things fun. I promise you they will get multiple crowns in heaven for their hard, thankless work!

Maybe you find yourself serving God in ways that are also demanding, thankless, and make you wish you had a different role from the season you're in. Maybe the work you've been assigned to isn't in line with your natural bent. But sometimes God calls us to work outside our gifting to learn something new about ourselves or others.

I've learned I'm not naturally a hospitable person. I love to host parties in order to socialize with others, but I don't love all the work that goes into the food prep or cleaning up. I also discovered I need a bit of variety in my routine every day instead of doing the same thing.

I loved the various roles I got to play at that camp and how I learned something about myself (and God) in each one. Some weekly roles I filled proved to be extremely hard for me and definitely weren't in my natural skill set. One week I was put on the maintenance crew and tasked with chopping down trees. Not easy, especially when you're one of the smallest girls on the crew. Some of the roles didn't fulfill me in ways mentoring as a camp counselor did. But I still saw so much purpose in each task, each role. No matter the role, we had to work together as the body of Christ to facilitate His Kingdom's work.

I also learned a lot about humility—working for God in ways that went unseen by others but were seen by God. It taught me to put others before myself and appreciate the work that goes on behind the scenes. It helped me to realize that there are seasons when God will call you to do something outside your comfort zone or outside your natural gifts, which probably won't be glamorous work! But it all serves a purpose.

It also taught me that taking advantage of the free soft-serve ice cream provided for staff members will make your pants burst by the end of the summer!

The cultivating and pruning God did in my heart those first two summers prepared me for another cultivating of the heart the following summer.

* * *

I've never felt worthy of Jeff. Even when we first started dating, I remember my new Christian girlfriends were in awe that this solid Christian guy wanted to date a post–wild sorority party girl turned Christian. He was the homecoming king of his high school, a favorite of many. I was intimidated by his deep knowledge of the Bible (and my lack thereof) and in awe of the fact that in two years of dating, he actually wanted to marry me—someone who was still growing in her faith with a scarlet past. He assured me my past iniquities were as white as snow to him. If Jesus forgave me, he could forgive me as well and look past the damage I had done to myself. "Therefore, if anyone is in Christ, he is a new creation. The old has passed away; behold, the new has come" (2 Cor. 5:17, ESV). I was a new creation.

I know, I know. You're probably wondering how to get a guy like this. Honestly, I don't know. In fact, I pushed him away a few times in our relationship and messed up many times when we were together. I thought for sure he wouldn't stick around with this mess of a girl. But he continued to pursue me. Kind of like the story of Hosea and Gomer. Do you know that story? You need to, so stay with me.

It's a rather miraculous story. God told a man named Hosea to marry a promiscuous woman, a prostitute, named Gomer. This wasn't just any sort of promiscuous woman. She was a woman with absolutely no hope or chance of marrying a decent guy. Think about it: a godly man marrying a prostitute. This would make national headlines and for sure produce a reality TV show next to *The Hills*. Regardless of her past and current predicament, Hosea pursued her and married her. I'm sure Gomer was in shock and awe that this amazing guy wanted her. You would think it would stop her bad habits, but it didn't. Gomer continued to run away, pursuing the life she knew before, likely to the brothels where she once was, leaving Hosea over and over again.

If you were Hosea, what would you do? Give up? Plaster the news on Facebook and try to wreck her life? Move on to someone else with a better pedigree? This would be a more normal reaction to this kind of thing. That's what the world expects us to do.

But the miraculous part of this story? Hosea kept going after Gomer. God told him to keep bringing her back, so he did.

Can you imagine? I mean this is like the epitome of a modern-day soap opera.

The most radical part was that Hosea extended forgiveness toward Gomer. Not just once. Not just twice. But multiple times. It was a totally uncharacteristic action for any person to do in this type of situation. It demonstrates an unconditional love that can come only from knowing the love and forgiveness of Jesus. I can only imagine how Gomer felt about all of this—torn between the extravagant love by this man, her husband, who loved her unconditionally, and the earth-shattering guilt of feeling unworthy of this great love.

Putting myself in her shoes, I would run away too with how loud my own self-condemning thoughts would be, feeling completely undeserving of this kind of love or relationship.

In some ways, I identified with Gomer. I felt Jeff deserved better. I believed the lie that I was too broken, too damaged, and not worthy of him. But Jeff wouldn't have it. He stuck with me until he made me his.

And Hosea wouldn't have it either. He loved Gomer, despite her disobedience and sinful past and present mistakes.

Friend, I don't know your story or your present situation. But you aren't too broken or too messed up to be worthy of love. And while the deep love of another person is truly incredible to experience, it is nothing, and I mean nothing, in comparison with the fathomless love and grace of God. Your Heavenly Father is never going to give up on you. He will never stop pursuing you and will never stop loving you, even when you feel like all is lost.

Along with the love high I experienced when I got engaged, I was still on a "spiritual high" with God three years into my new faith. Just as I thought my feelings for the man I was going to marry would never change, I thought this spiritual high with God would never end.

But as marriage, careers, and babies came along, I felt my heart grow cold. My excitement for Jesus and His love waned. Worship felt like empty words. Church was okay, and I did all the things I was "supposed to do" as a Christian, but I wondered if this was really all there was to God. Where did the extravagant beauty and wonder of God go? Where was the thrill of experiencing His Spirit moving in me? Did I miss something?

Ultimately, I asked the question, *Why doesn't this spiritual high last?*

* * *

If you've been a Christian for a few years, you know what I'm talking about. We've all experienced this at some point. There's a reason for it that took some exploring to discover.

I was twenty-nine when I noticed that my soul had grown cold and stagnant, despite God so powerfully showing up in that college bedroom of mine ten years earlier. My nineteen-month-old twins in diapers toddled around me while my giant belly prepared for their baby sister to arrive at any moment. Signs of Christmas were sprinkled about our home as we waited for her debut (very much a sprinkle, not a downpour due to this season of twin exhaustion). Although signs of joy were all around me, I wondered where the joy inside me had gone.

But something stirred in me in the fall of 2013. At the women's retreat, I felt a stirring in my heart that Jesus was and is still alive within me, despite how I felt. There I met my spiritual and licensed counselor. She was a godsend—a wealth of knowledge and Biblical wisdom and a heart for the Lord that was palpable. She began the process of thawing my heart, breaking open the ice fortress that had slowly encased it over the years. It took some chiseling. The ice pack had grown so thick over my heart it would take more than a few sessions to break it all down.

The layers had to do with the lies I believed about God, views that were not quite right, which filtered into how I viewed the world and myself. It clouded my lens, making everything look heavier, darker, and unfulfilling. I allowed certain unhealthy issues to creep into my daily life, things I didn't think were a big deal that were actually preventing me from experiencing deeper intimacy with God. I became despondent about the Christian faith, and although I still believed in God, I often wondered, *What happened to that fire I used to have for Him? What really is the purpose to my life? Is life just about having babies, decorating my home with stuff, and going to church every Sunday? What happened to the relationship I used to have with Him?*

It seemed like God was a flame that had slowly burned out, like a match, only good for a brief while until real life settled in—without any kindling to keep the fire going. And maybe that is just the way the Christian life was meant to be...

Friend, what I didn't realize is that a certain kind of kindling is required to keep the flame in your heart growing. Sustainable wood is necessary to bring a steady, warm burn. And if you want a long-lasting fire, add some coal to the embers, and it will last throughout the night, long enough for you to stoke the flame the next morning to bring it to a roar again. Everyone knows a real fire is hotter and lasts longer than the strike of a single match.

I didn't keep stoking that fire in my heart. I kept lighting spiritual matches—enjoying a great sermon but failing to apply it to my daily life. Attending various churches without regularity because I was always frustrated with something, unable to find the perfect church (hint: there is no perfect church). Reading the Bible but failing to stay consistent.

I needed to not just believe in God but live out my faith like He is for real.

In 2013, a few months into my new soul-searching, I read a passage that fundamentally changed my view. It's about how we grow spiritually and why this spiritual high isn't meant to last forever: "I fed you with milk, not solid food, for you were not ready for it" (1 Cor. 3:2, ESV).

Picture this image: an adult nursing off their adult mother's breast. Sorry for the imagery. It's not a pleasant sight to think about, right? Nobody would do this. But that's the point! Have you seen a grown adult live off milk alone? Do they just whip out a bottle of milk for every meal or ask their mom for more from their breast and feel satisfied? I sure hope not! And yet I believe this is the current spiritual state of many—unable or unwilling to cross over to eat solid food.

I nursed three babies (two at the same time, mind you) and saw their growth through something as simple but deeply nourishing as the milk from my breast. However, as they reached the six-month stage, it was clear they were ready to be introduced to pureed and soft solid foods. Their teeth grew, allowing harder foods to be introduced, which was suitable for their growing bodies. Even now, at their six-year-old state, I still cut up their meat to help them digest it better, because they can't physically cut it themselves yet.

This complementary verse encourages this concept about how we are meant to grow spiritually: "Like newborn infants, long for the pure spiritual milk, that by it you may grow up into salvation—if indeed you have tasted that the Lord is good" (1 Peter 2:2–3, ESV).

In the beginning, I was like a baby in my faith. God abundantly poured into me spiritual milk that my heart and soul absolutely needed and longed for in that season. A milk-induced high continued and sustained me for many years as I soaked in all the new things I was learning about Jesus. I finally tasted and saw that the Lord is good (Psalm 34:8). I experienced a rich relationship as I fully depended on Him like an infant would. God nurtured me with tangible expressions of His love through Spirit-infused worship, increased my awe of Him with every passage I read, and nurtured my heart through tangible Spirit-infused circumstances.

But time passes, you reach another milestone, and things start to shift, right? Worship loses a bit of its luster. Sermons don't pack a punch like they used to. The newness of it all begins to fade and the realities of some hard truths start to challenge you in ways you hadn't anticipated. Friends move away and loneliness returns. Marriage gets hard. You become stretched too thin by unpaid bills piling up, and the diagnosis doesn't go away no matter how hard you've prayed. You forget to read the Word because it starts to feel boring to you. Or it pierces your pride in ways that hurt. I don't like pain either. You don't understand God's will. And there are so many qualified theologians who fall on completely opposite sides of the spectrum in what they claim is true that it becomes overwhelming to try to figure it all out. You'd rather not dig into it anymore or share your faith because it divides your family, causes tension on Facebook, and being the peacemaker that you are, you'd rather just quietly float through life. It seems easier to become numb to the American Christian machine rather than letting God see where your faith is lacking, where your heart is hurting, and allowing Him to revive your heart again.

The problem is, you are not meant to live off mother's milk forever. When you do, your faith weakens, and spiritual maturity is lost.

The spiritual high isn't meant to last, friend. God in His mercy isn't going to spoon-feed us forever. Wouldn't that be silly if you were still being spoon-fed and trying to get all of your nourishment from milk alone? He is weaning us from this spiritual milk for a reason. He wants us to move over to solid spiritual foods, cultivating deeper awareness of Him, which will promote an exhilarating, intoxicating, revitalizing faith in the things we believe. We don't let our own children continue drinking mother's milk forever; we help broaden their palate and prepare their growing bodies for the nourishment they need to sustain themselves.

In the same way we encourage certain foods, we limit certain foods as well. Not everything is encouraged or allowed into our bodies. Some things have now been found to promote cancer, increase toxins in your liver, and a host of other unwanted things. In the same way, God puts boundaries on certain things we might want to include in our life because He knows they will cause more harm than good. This is something to keep in mind as you ponder what you're allowing in your life and whether it is healthy or unhealthy for you.

Is it possible that you are feeling stuck because you haven't moved over to the deeper, more sustainable spiritual nourishment you need to revive your heart and release your purpose? Have you cut out or refined what's holding you back from deeper restored intimacy with God? Are you restoring your heart and mind with solid, healthy spiritual nourishment for your soul? Are you wanting a deeper, more intimate relationship with God but you're unwilling to discipline yourself to reach a spiritual maturity that makes you more alive, because what used to sustain you won't anymore? The spiritual high *isn't* meant to last forever. It's time now that you feast on solid foods.

* * *

I could see the instructor's lips moving, but no sound could be heard above the drone of the engine and the howling wind from the open hatch. However, I was pretty sure, reading his lips, he said, "Are you ready?"

I felt him yank on the straps to double-check. These straps held my back tightly against his chest, which I didn't mind, because he was the one with the parachute who would save me from this fall, a fall I was initiating.

Staring through the open hatch at fifteen thousand feet of open air below, I readied myself for the plunge. Skydiving isn't for the faint of heart. The scariest part is always the leap, right? I mean, who in their right mind willingly jumps out of an airplane fifteen thousand feet above the ground? Even with a parachute, there's always that off chance that it won't open, initiating your own death.

After a few seconds, I hit terminal velocity, which basically feels like you are floating on air. Everything moved slowly even though I was speeding 120 miles per hour toward the ground. It was almost peaceful in some ways. The drone of the wind ripping past my ears was like a sound machine lulling me to sleep. Except there was no way I would sleep through this moment—indescribable and worth the death-defying experience! My instructor literally had my back. I trusted and believed he would get us both safely to the ground. Because if not, he would crash and die along with me, right? What good would that do for either of us?

So much of our spiritual walk is like this. We like to play it safe by staying on the ground, even though Jesus is beckoning us to an indescribable adventure with Him. God is inviting us into things with Him, but often we aren't willing to join Him. Or maybe we've said yes to Him, but when it comes to taking that leap, we chicken out and don't trust He really has our back. Perhaps we've actually leaped, and the parachute didn't open, leaving us crashing to the ground in pieces. What then?

I have answers to these scenarios. But it takes some time to unpack it all. So stay with me to the end to see what I've discovered through my own crash-and-burn experiences with God.

First, let's look at Peter, a man I think we should give a little more credit to. Peter was a disciple who walked with the living, breathing Jesus. One night he was in a boat with a bunch of his other disciple buddies making their way to the next location on their journey of faith. It became incredibly windy on the sea, winds whipping the water into whitecaps. Likely they hunkered down in safety on the little boat, unable to do much except wait it out until it ceased, praying they wouldn't sink. Darkness was upon them as they tossed and turned on the stormy sea.

At one point, I imagine Peter decided they should check things out above deck. We don't know the exact details, but based on his character, it would seem to fit. Peter may have worked to build up the courage to peek above the cabin of the ship, perhaps to check the ropes and sails to see if they were still intact. Or maybe he was checking to see if they could locate land yet. Bracing himself in the wind and rain, I imagine he popped open the ship hatch only to see he needed help on deck. His buddies came up with him, checking to make sure all was secure while they were getting tossed and sprayed by the wind-churned sea. Suddenly they noticed something on the water moving toward them. It was hard to tell what it was. At first, they thought it was a ghost floating on the water. (That makes sense, because what human walks on water?) But as the figure came closer, this "ghost," noticing their fear, spoke: "Take courage, it is I! Don't be afraid" (Matthew 14:27).

Jesus. Jesus's voice broke through the crackling storm. A voice of power, peace, and purpose beyond the normal voice of any man. But even with the sound of Jesus's voice, the disciples were still afraid and unsure. Peter finally had the courage to ask this figure on the water something, one of the boldest moves ever recorded in Scripture. He asked, "Lord, if it's you...tell me to come to you on the water" (Matthew 14:28).

Seriously? Who in their right mind would think of something like this? Not only was Peter willing to speak up and talk to Jesus amid the wind and storm, but he also had the guts to take a huge leap of faith, asking Jesus to do the impossible through him by enabling him to walk on water. And maybe, just maybe, Peter sensed that this was what He was supposed to do.

Regardless, the impossible was made possible as Peter experienced walking on water toward Jesus. And not on a sea as flat as glass. Ripping and roaring waves and wind lurched at him to drag him down into the depths below. This moment was likely the most incredible moment of Peter's life. I can almost see the look on the other disciples' faces, their mouths hanging open, watching in awe from the safety of their boat.

Peter was willing to leave the safety of the boat to walk through the rolling waves, strong wind, and darkness toward a man who claimed he was Jesus. He was ready to do something completely terrifying and exhilarating, not to mention impossible without Jesus's help, because He's the one who makes the impossible possible (Matthew 19:26).

Here's the thing: I think God wants all of us to experience this with Him. But I wonder if we are too comfortable in our self-made boats.

* * *

I don't know how to say this next part without sounding insensitive or negative, but it needs to be stated. There's a certain cruise-ship Christianity that has poisoned our church culture in the United States and some other countries as well. I think it looks a lot like building a fleet of shiny cruise ships because it's a lot safer and more comfortable staying in those giant party ships than accepting God's invitation to venture toward uncomfortable places.

To be honest, cruise-ship Christianity has its perks. But it misses the boat to create soul-stirring faith.

While I believed in Jesus and accepted his gift of salvation, I was still playing it safe when it came to actively living out my faith. I attended church, listened to the sermons, sometimes shared a little about Jesus with others, but my life was pretty similar to the lives of my friends down the street who had no faith in God.

We like to fit in, don't we? We enjoy comfortable. Often, we hear a need presented by someone at church and say, "Oh, no! But that's someone else's responsibility" or "I can't do that because I'm a mom of young kids."

I used to make these excuses too to explain why I couldn't serve, even though I felt a tug in my heart.

On the opposite side of the spectrum, there are some of us doing too much and burning out for Jesus. You may be one of them, exhausted by your commitments to serve and overwhelmed by the amount of responsibility you have. You say yes to anything, pouring your heart into everything, leaving no room for soul-filling because you're pouring out faster than you're pouring in. Serving for Jesus may be breaking you instead of fulfilling you; you may be carrying more weight than God has called you to carry. Is it possible God is asking you to just *be* instead of *do* at this time?

I've experienced this. However, I believe most of us stay in the safety of our little boat, forgoing the thrilling adventure God is inviting us to embark on with Him. As Christians, we are too busy playing Candy Crush with our Christian friends, content in our little Christian bubble, taking no notice of those who are encountering Jesus in a different way. Or maybe you've glanced up from time to time and caught a glimpse of this wonder, a water-walking moment of awe for the girl walking on water with Him. You think, *Wow, how cool! I could never do that, though...*

But you can. You need to. Whatever God is calling you to do, you need to do that. Or whatever you're supposed to say no to, say no because this allows you to say yes to the best and most important yeses you are meant to pursue. Lysa TerKeurst says it well: "Whenever you say yes to something, there is less of you for something else. Make sure your yes is worth the less."[1]

When you're saying, "I could never do that..." what you're doing right now is drinking that bottle of milk, putting your ship on cruise control, allowing your heart and mind to grow stagnant. The nourishing of your faith is lacking. Denying His invitations, you allow complacency to destroy the vibrant relationship you are meant to taste with Him. You allow subtle issues to separate you from Him.

But what are those subtle issues? If they're so subtle and seemingly minor, does it really matter? Can't you just shrug them off?

You can. You have been. But you shouldn't anymore. To get to where you want to be—reviving your heart to release your purpose—this is where you need to go, friend, to revive your heart with confidence, passion, and zest for God as you refine away the lies that are holding you back.

Borrow This Reviving Prayer
When Words Are Few

God, I know You love me. Help me see that. Help me
believe that You have a path and plan for me. Help
me start pursuing You with my whole heart, not just
half a heart in the safety of my boat. I want to want
You more. Revive my heart to pursue You more
deeply, intentionally, and openly. I want to
experience the depth of Your love. I want to notice
where I'm lacking so that I can draw nearer to You.
In Jesus's name, amen.

Section 2

REFINE

I will bring that group through the fire and make them pure. I will refine them like silver and purify them like gold. They will call on my name, and I will answer them. I will say, "These are my people," and they will say, "The LORD is our God."

Zechariah 13:9, NLT

CHAPTER 4

Friends without Benefits

I quietly ate my food, not knowing how to join the conversation—uncomfortable as they ripped into the character of a girl in our class whom I thought they were friends with.

Glancing around the room, I picked up on the murmur of other conversations floating between booths and tables of food. Some were laughing, some serious, a few with few words to speak. It made me wonder how many of these people were offhandedly speaking poorly about another person they knew.

I've always wanted to be with the "in" crowd. Acceptance is an ardent desire of mine. These girls were the classic popular ones of the class. They were trendy, pretty, and somehow they took a liking to me as well. We had all graduated now, were working in our field of study, some with babies on the way. We all shared faith in God. However, the depth of their faith felt different from mine.

In fact, it seemed like God was more of an accessory in their lives, not a necessity.

Honestly, I had been in that same boat too. But things were starting to change. My heart was beginning to notice the subtle offenses we were making.

"Seriously, she is so annoying, and I can't believe how hyper she is!"

They all chimed in, in agreement, while the ringleader raged on and on about her. I tried to change the topic.

"So, have you had any interesting situations happen at work this week?"

While this did change the topic, soon they were ripping on what the patients were wearing and finally got onto the subject of toes.

"I have a feet fetish. I know, I know, but I can't stand not having polish on my feet. And seeing people with undone toes? Ewwww! It disgusts me."

I sheepishly curled my bare toes under, hiding them deeper into my peep-toe shoes. For the first time I noticed that each of theirs were perfectly manicured and freshly polished.

The impact these conversations was having on me didn't dawn on me until my husband voiced it one day. I had just returned from another lunch meet-up, apparently ringing out onto my husband the discontent that I had soaked up from the group. "You're always complaining about something when you come back from hanging out with those girls," he piped up.

"No, I don't!" I defended my position, even though in

the back of my mind I knew there was some truth to what he said.

He started gently responding to my rebuttals. "Listen to yourself speak. You're complaining that the house isn't big enough; you need a new purse even though you have five good ones and only use one; you're talking negatively about yourself and others... In fact, you're really negative... you seem so discontented with everything."

He was right. I couldn't help but think of the verse speaking so clearly in this moment: "Don't criticize one another, brothers and sisters. Anyone who defames or judges a fellow believer defames and judges the law. If you judge the law, you are not a doer of the law but a judge" (James 4:11, CSB).

There are multiple verses that speak directly to this topic of gossiping and criticizing one another. You know it's unhealthy. You wouldn't say those things to her face. Well, maybe you would, and that's another issue you need to wrestle with. You get caught up in the banter, though, not seeing the invisible harm it's doing to your heart and soul. You brush it off like it's no big deal.

But it is a big deal. The enemy is sneaky, making you think that what you're doing causes no harm and it's impossible to stop anyway, so why try?

I hear this talk around church too, in discipleship class or among other women's groups. I hear this at the gym, in the Chick-fil-A line, and at park benches. I see it blasted all over social media, although the Facebook unfollow button has been a helpful filter for this.

It hurts to admit I get caught up in this too. I get fired up in the moment and let words loose that I wouldn't let loose in the face of the woman I'm talking about. I "go with the flow," thinking that this isn't directly associating myself with the deadly banter, and yet my nodding or even quiet silence speaks acceptance of this behavior instead of putting a cork in it.

I should have confronted those women during one of our many lunches. I tried to change the subject or redirect them in a joking way: "Okay, okay, enough now..." when the poisonous banter was too much. But listen, I'm no saint. I joined in the banter often. I got caught up in the negative talk too. I coveted with them, envied others with them, and didn't think much of it at the time.

But God continued to penetrate my heart, whispering in my mind, "This isn't healthy, and you know it. I've created you for more than this."

Perhaps if I held more authority and leadership in the group, I could have initiated positive change in them. Maybe I could have been bolder and stronger in my approach to stop it, but the truth is I was being pulled into the struggle.

You may not be able to change the cause for everyone, but you may be able to cause a change for yourself.

This was made clear one day when I came home from another meet-up feeling deflated. "You know, Jeff," I began, "I think it's becoming unhealthy for me to hang out with those girls. I can't change their behavior, and it's hurting me more than helping me. I want authentic conversations about deeper things. I'm realizing more and more I just don't relate to them like I hoped I would."

Jeff's smile said it all. He knew what I knew all along. I needed to cut ties with these friends to allow a closer tie with God.

Maybe you're thinking, *But, Rachel, aren't we called to love others, even love our enemies? Aren't we called to be a friend to others and lead them to Jesus? Aren't we called to be a light to them and stay friends with them, regardless of the sacrifice and hurt it brings us?*

Some of this is true, but there are lies within these statements too. Yes, we are called to love others, even our enemies. Yes, we are to lead others to Jesus. Yes, we are to be a light to this world and not shy away from our royal identity. But no, we are not to be friends at the expense of taking out our own hearts and minds in the process, becoming entangled and ensnared in their sinful ways. We need to put proper boundaries in place, even with our enemies, which sometimes looks like cutting off all contact for the protection of your heart and theirs. We need to remember this verse: "Make no friendship with a man given to anger, nor go with a wrathful man, lest you learn his ways and entangle yourself in a snare" (Prov. 22:24–25, ESV). We aren't meant to save everyone; that's Jesus's job. He will send someone else in your place to love them like Jesus when you cannot. It's okay to admit this friendship or group of friends isn't healthy anymore. You can cut ties with their influence in your life. By not doing so you may be preventing a deeper, more joy-filled connection with

God. You may be missing out on other ways He wants to use your influence for His glory.

* * *

Call it what you want: anger, bitterness, slander, deceitfulness, coveting, speaking unkindly about others. It's all the same. We need to be careful of who we make friends with because of the detriment it can create to our hearts and minds. God wants us to experience love, peace, thoughtfulness, kindness, and joy in our lives. What's holding you back from experiencing this? It could be the relationships around you.

I was becoming entangled through this group. I was ensnared. I didn't realize it at the time. I thought I was strong enough to be a positive influence over them. But I couldn't. I saw the damaging effects my association with this group of friends was having on my walk with God. I didn't have influence in the group to make an impactful change. I had to separate myself even though I was torn by the decision. It wasn't easy. I still had one friend in the group I really wanted to stay connected to. But it proved too hard. And through prayer, God made it clear that though I was giving up something big—a friend group—He was calling me into something so much *more*.

Friendships are a sticky business. It becomes even stickier as a Christian. Especially when we read verses like, "Love your enemies, do good to those who hate you, bless those who curse you, pray for those who mistreat you"

(Luke 6:27–28). But what we fail to realize is that loving our enemies and being friends with them are totally different categories. So many of us get in this place where we believe we must sacrifice our health, our minds, our souls for the sake of being friends with those who are corrupting our character. But God has a lot to say about friendships: "Do not be misled: 'Bad company corrupts good character'" (1 Cor. 15:33).

Our environment plays a huge role in how our character continues to form. God states that we should not be misled about our understanding in choosing friends. You do have a choice. You don't have to be a scapegoat for others, and you aren't always meant to play the role of the influencer in the group. Saving your character is more important than securing your connection to those who are bringing you down.

Pretend you're a recovering alcoholic. You know all the bars in town. All the bartenders know you by name. You've been in recovery for a year, and someone you want to cultivate a friendship with asks you to go to the bars with them. Hesitating, you say yes. At the bar, you order a soda water but everyone else next to you is sipping or pounding down the drinks. People you know give you a rowdy hug with, "Say, haven't seen you in a while! Where've you been?" They notice what you're drinking and ask what's changed.

"I'm just not up for drinking tonight," you say. But they won't take it. Suddenly, you have free beer and a shot of tequila ready and waiting that's been ordered for you. Feeling the pressure to fit in, thinking, *I'll be fine, it's just one drink,* you pound the tequila and sip the beer, noticing how good it tastes again. But soon, one drink turns into two, and next thing you know, you're pulled into the swirling matrix of intoxication.

For some of us, the pull may be too strong to handle. It may be forty years later, and you know entering the bar will be a temptation too great.

Some relationships are just too damaging to salvage or reenter because they could completely destroy us. It can even be with a Christian friend, but the blood you both drew is too much. I believe in working to make amends. I believe we are called to press in. But I believe there comes a time when letting go is the best thing for the relationship.

I also believe in the Word of God that says to be careful what we allow into our lives. Be careful whom we associate ourselves with. You are worth more than the demise of your soul through the slander, negativity, and detriment they could bring to your life. Be careful not to settle, because God has so many life-giving relationships He wants to introduce you to.

So cut ties with those who you know are leading you toward corruption. In this way, God is more gloriously magnified.

* * *

I'm thirty-six and still navigating this whole friendship issue. I'm still figuring out how to find healthy friends while still being a friend to those He has called me to befriend. It all seems a delicate balance—having enough friends to positively influence my life while having a few project friends to work on. As my influence online grows, I feel the weight of that more as I'm connected to more and more people whom I feel responsible for positively influencing.

But the truth is, it's literally impossible for you and me to be everyone's friend. While this may seem like common sense, my brain needs to read this again. Because the way I've been wired, I want to be everyone's friend. God can do the impossible, but there are certain scientific human limitations, like having a limited capacity to be friends with everyone and fulfill the needs of every person.

But Jesus can.

Seriously, ponder that for a moment. Through the Holy Spirit, God can connect with each of us and fulfill our every need. His Word attests to this (Psalm 91:14, Jeremiah 1:5, John 10:14). God likens knowing each of us to a shepherd knowing his sheep and calling them each by name. This was a powerful illustration at the time. Multiple articles today discuss the truth of this illustration: "The modern shepherd...has a wonderful memory, which retains the name of every sheep. The flocks sometimes contain several hundred, and yet each one has a name and the shepherd knows it, and calls every sheep by its proper name...[One observer] tells of watching shepherds with flocks upon the slopes of Mount Hermon: 'Each shepherd...trains his sheep to come at his call, to go in order, in twos or fours, in squares and circles; one from the outer circle in a flock of a thousand will come when its name is called.' It is the voice of the shepherd that the sheep recognizes."[1]

I have to remind myself of this truth: that God knows me by name. He is my loving Shepherd. He is my best friend. He has been with me during the darkest moments of my life and He has continued to fight for me and believes the best in me despite the countless mistakes I make. He is refining and restoring my life to more closely reflect His image, drawing me closer to Him as I follow the sound of His voice.

Often, we see glimpses of God's presence when we look back at those hard moments in our life. When we've lost a friend, been betrayed by a friend, or had to cut ties with a friend, that's when God does incredible soul work in us. He helps us recognize our need for Him as our ultimate friend. He comforts our heart in ways that are indescribable. He restores our hearts from the earthshattering pains of friendship losses or hurtful relationship responses by extending His unconditional love and forgiveness over us.

I think we are constantly searching for fulfillment in the wrong places. We believe in the lie that a friendship or relationship will fully fill that lonely ache in our hearts. We hold on to bad relationships because we fear the emptiness more than the hurt this person is bringing to our life.

We keep asking God the question, "Do You love me?"

And when He responds, "Yes," we aren't convinced and say with more fervor, "No, do You *really* love me, God?"

He gently and patiently responds to our pleas, "Yes, don't you see how much I love you? I've painted vast metallic sunsets for you that are filled with golds, crimsons, and violets to demonstrate my love for you. I've been the footsteps in the sinking sand carrying you when you couldn't carry yourself any longer. I'm the peace that surpasses understanding when life doesn't work out the way you want it to. I sacrificed my life for you, so you can have yours. But do you choose to love Me too? I cannot make you love Me. I can only show you the love I have for you. So, my question for you is, 'Do you *really* love Me?'"

Saying you love someone isn't quite as powerful as demonstrating that love through actions. You can prove your love for someone based on how you treat them and how you seek to love them in the ways they like to be loved.

When we say, "I love You, God," but then gossip with our girlfriends about how annoying Jill is, or when we seek friendships to fill the ache in our heart more than God Himself, we're rejecting God's love for us. When we treat others poorly, especially online, or think we are better than another, condemning instead of commending, we are forgetting how much God loves us and them too. We reject instead of accept. Retaliate instead of compensate. Judge others instead of love them.

To love God is to love Him in the ways He asks us to love: "Love is patient and kind; love does not envy or boast; it is not arrogant or rude. It does not insist on its own way; it is not irritable or resentful; it does not rejoice at wrongdoing, but rejoices with the truth. Love bears all things, believes all things, hopes all things, endures all things. Love never ends" (1 Cor. 13:4–8, ESV).

We will never be perfect at seeking God's love and loving Him perfectly in return. We will still revert to our natural ways, looking for love from others in ways only God can fill. But this is the refine and restore process: refining away the lies and restoring our hearts and minds to what is true, to break free from the subtle sins in your life, such as gossiping or engaging in negative actions with others, and restore your heart through friendships that build up instead of tear down. Make it your life's mission to listen when He calls you back to His love, searching for you by name, and leave the herd to run into His loving arms. Because this is who God is: Our Protector. Our Director. Our Refiner. He will enable you to become a better version of yourself if you will only let Him.

Borrow This Refining Prayer When Words Are Few

Father God, breaking to the surface of my mind are friendships I see that are toxic to me right now. I see where I've been gossiping, faltering, and been unloving toward others, emphasized through these friendships. If I need to break away from these friends because of the negative impact overflowing into my life, give me a sign from You and the courage to take action. I know I need to build stronger friendships with those who will uplift me, encourage me, and are trustworthy. Help me fall more and more in love with You so I can be a better, more loving friend to others, especially those You want me to cultivate more deeply than most. In Jesus's name, amen.

CHAPTER 5

American Idols

Most women dream about having babies and getting married. I dreamed of being financially successful in a lucrative career, retired by the age of thirty.

I know. So humble.

So when I heard about this network marketing company that claimed it would help me do just that, I was all in. Being a persistent person who doesn't give up easily, I pushed through the hurdles I faced in this company for three years: cold calls, product parties, rejection after rejection after rejection. I poured in thousands of dollars guaranteed to "make my business successful," to no avail. I sank into a deep depression after this long season, part of this due to my relentless pursuit of money and failing miserably in the process.

For the record, I don't think all network marketing companies are evil. However, I can't help but notice how this industry and other businesses like it are leading a lot of Christians astray regarding what God actually says about money. I hear the statement over and over again, "The most important gain in life is financial security." While financial security can be a great gift, it can also be to our greatest detriment.

Being a young and immature Christian, I believed God wanted me to be successful with my network marketing business so I could invest in His Kingdom work while enjoying a cushioned life at the same time. But what I failed to realize at the time was how much my heart struggled with worshipping money, stuff, and esteem over God Himself. I was abusing God's promises of "good things" for me through the false belief that God wanted me to be financially successful.

The truth is, God doesn't promise financial success. If this were true, what does this mean for Christians in first-world countries struggling just to make ends meet? Do they have less faith? Did God forget about them?

God didn't and hasn't forgotten about them. He hasn't forgotten about you. We forget that financial success isn't the primary goal in life. This mind-set can lead to a whole cacophony of heart, mind, and soul issues. Multiple verses point to this truth. Here's just one: "Better the little that the righteous have than the wealth of many wicked" (Psalm 37:16).

Having a "little," God says, can be better than having a lot, because much can create wickedness in our hearts. It can make us arrogant, prideful, and selfish. This is not who God wants us to become.

Here's another passage that speaks plainly to this: "Command those who are rich in this present world not to be arrogant nor to put their hope in wealth, which is so uncertain, but to put their hope in God, who richly provides us with everything for our enjoyment. Command them to do good, to be rich in good deeds, and to be generous and willing to share. In this way they will lay up treasure for themselves as a firm foundation for the coming age, so that they may take hold of the life that is truly life" (1 Timothy 6:7–9).

God unpacks a lot for us in this passage. I want to highlight the part that says God does not want us to put our hope in wealth. God desires that we put our hope in Him, not in the wealth of the world. Hope means to look with expectancy, to depend and to count on. We are not to become so focused on securing wealth that we forget the true wealth of what we gain in the security of God alone. When we pursue God over wealth, God enables us to be generous in good deeds, which is far greater than having financial security in life.

And yet this is easier said than done.

* * *

I watched in horror the video my friend posted about my hometown, Paradise, California. In late 2018, the most destructive and most deadly fire in California history broke out, and my friend, my parents, brother, sister, and their families fled for their lives. There was little to no warning that the fire was coming, raging out of control. Only through word of mouth did anyone know to evacuate. They barely made it out alive.

Flames soared to the skies as hundred-year-old pine trees lining both sides of the road went up like they'd been blow-torched. Fireballs and flaming branches hit car windows as people fled through smoke so dense they could hardly see where they were going. It was just before noon, and yet it looked to be midnight with the smoke clouding out every ray of sunlight.

My sister's home burned down completely, along with thousands of other homes in my hometown that used to be filled with 27,000 people. Only six weeks prior I had been sitting in her cozy living room commenting on her cute end table that was really a fancy type of trash bucket flipped upside down. Trust me, it definitely looked better as an end table. Our kids pulled out her toy bin holding feet of train tracks, placing multiple trains on her carpet where they played for hours. Her massive floor-to-ceiling wall of books in her living room, a collection that had taken years and thousands of dollars to build, was my favorite element in her home.

Now all that's left are ash and smoke, a semblance of her front entryway still standing, the frames of her washer and dryer, and the casing of a lone wheelbarrow in the front yard.

While they have insurance to compensate for some of the losses, there are priceless mementos they just can't re-create—heirlooms, saved baby items, older photo books from before Instagram. Losing everything is devastating. And yet, I admire her continual positive attitude. "It's just stuff. We can rebuild. We are simply thankful to be alive and have each other," she reassured me.

She still has days of tears for what was lost (and so do I), but this sits as a great reminder of what's truly most important in life. It's not our stuff. It's not what we build here on this earth. It's the relationships we have with each other and our faith that sustains us when all else turns to ash and smoke.

Have you ever heard the saying, "You can't take it with you"? At times this expression can be annoying (like when my husband sees me coveting a Pottery Barn couch), but it's true. The stuff we collect here in life, the money we save up, the trinkets we hold so near and dear to us won't be taken with us when we pass from this life into the next.

Although my sister has no choice but to face the reality of her loss, I can't help but think of what would happen if we were asked to choose this willingly—to give up all our monetary possessions—to follow Jesus. Could you do this? Would you?

There's a relevant story in Mark 10. Let's read what it says together: "Just then a man came up to Jesus and asked, 'Teacher, what good thing must I do to get eternal life?'

"'Why do you ask me about what is good?' Jesus replied. 'There is only One who is good. If you want to enter life, keep the commandments.'

"'Which ones?' he inquired.

"Jesus replied, 'You shall not murder, you shall not commit adultery, you shall not steal, you shall not give false testimony, honor your father and mother,' and 'love your neighbor as yourself.'

"'All these I have kept,' the young man said. 'What do I still lack?'

"Jesus answered, 'If you want to be perfect, go, sell your possessions and give to the poor, and you will have treasure in heaven. Then come, follow me.'

"When the young man heard this, he went away sad, because he had great wealth.

"Then Jesus said to his disciples, 'Truly I tell you, it is hard for someone who is rich to enter the kingdom of heaven. Again, I tell you, it is easier for a camel to go through the eye of a needle than for someone who is rich to enter the kingdom of God'" (Mark 10:17–31).

Let me be real with you: I don't love this story. It makes me question my desire for quartz countertops in my kitchen, my Coach purse purchases (even though I get them at 70 percent off), and all the Amazon boxes arriving at my house that my husband loves *so* much (don't you pretend you don't do this too). It makes me wonder if I'm giving enough to ministries, to the church, to those in need around me, and if I'm still being wise with my finances at the same time. It makes me question, "Where is my heart with money? Am I worshipping my stuff too much? Am I giving enough? If God asked me to give it all up, could I do this?"

Do you ever question this? Friend, this is a good thing to question. It's those who don't ask the question who worry me.

Too often, I think we turn a blind eye to our idol worship of stuff. We pretend we don't have an issue buying more than we need. We rack up our credit card debt because this is "normal." We buy a bigger house than we can afford because we can't tell our hearts no. We seek to impress others with what we drive or what we wear. We say, "Everyone else has it; I don't want to look out of place!" when our one-year-old phone is perfectly fine. We stuff our garages with boxes of trinkets we don't touch for twenty years. We strive for more, more, more, saying to ourselves, "Once I get to this monthly amount, I will give more generously to others for God's Kingdom."

We spend our whole lives striving to build up earthly riches when God's Word says, "Do not store up for yourselves treasures on earth, where moths and vermin destroy, and where thieves break in and steal" (Matt. 6:19). It also says, "For where your treasure is, there your heart will be also" (Matt. 6:21).

Where is your heart on this, friend? We need to honestly assess where our heart is with money because if we don't or refuse to, it will create greed and selfishness, and, worse, form a barrier between us and God. We tell God, "You can have everything, except…" instead of "God, I trust you with my finances! I will be a good steward of my money, and I will use it to bring more glory and honor to You!"

Yet I see many well-intentioned believers bringing more glory and honor to themselves through the money God has given them than using it in ways God desires it to be used. We glorify our bodies, our houses, our kids with it. We covet what we don't have. We get envious and jealous of the things of this world. I'm not an exception; I do this too.

But what about those who are good stewards of their money? Can you still be a good steward of money and be a wealthy Christian? Is money wrong or bad?

First, money isn't in and of itself bad. It's amoral—meaning it's neither good nor bad. It can be used for both. It all depends on the source from which it's being used. The source being—you, your heart. You need to assess where your heart is with money.

First Timothy 6:10 says, "The love of money is the root of all kinds of evil." When you love money more than relationships, especially your relationship with God, this can bring all kinds of evil to your heart and mind. Money itself isn't evil, but the love of it over God is.

I would be lying if I said I don't struggle with idolizing money, my stuff, or the "keeping up with the Joneses" mentality. I do. I *really* do. I'm challenged daily by this issue and am seeking daily to be refined and restored to the truth. But to say I haven't made progress in this area would also be a lie, because I've worked hard to overcome this heart issue.

There are a few things, practically speaking, that have helped me stop idolizing money and monetary items, and I think they can help you too:

1. **Head Check:** Stop acting like it's not a big deal. I think so many of us are numb to the negative effects that money and cherishing things is having on our hearts and minds. The problem with sloughing it off is that it becomes a breeding ground for weeds of greed and pride to take root in our lives, slowly choking us before we ever realize it. We need to admit this struggle first to ourselves, then to our Creator, then maybe to a

close friend. Remember, God loves you despite your struggle with this. He knows it's hard. But He loves a repentant and willing heart. He will help you understand where your areas of struggle with this are and convict you through the Holy Spirit and empower you to make positive changes in your life.

2. **Heart Check:** Let me speak plainly: if you can't practice the art of generosity now no matter how much money is in the bank, you won't be generous with your money later when you're finally "making it." Look, I'm no saint with this. I still struggle with the desire to have the finer things in life in a way that's unhealthy for my heart. Although money and stuff are neither good nor bad and we can definitely enjoy the benefits they bring to our lives, we must practice a heart of thankfulness and generosity. Saturate yourself with a new perspective. Let me give you one mind-blowing, life-changing perspective right now: the poorest in America are richer than 80 percent of the world. If you live in America, no matter your income status, you are already rich. Try that on for size and let it soak in. Be thankful, friend. And start with giving just five dollars per month to a cause, the church, or someone in need. I assure you, your heart will thank you for it.

3. **Hoard Check:** Do you have too much stuff? Look around you. Your stuff could be preventing you from

doing the things God has invited you to do with Him.
For my family and me, it became clear that my husband needed to quit his successful job and sell our
gorgeous home in Southern California. It was necessary to enable the work God was calling us to do,
though we didn't even know what the work was at
the time. We just knew He told us to go. So we went,
and figured it out along the way. We are still figuring it out, still wondering what other job God will call
my husband to as we live on less and live off of my
salary alone. But God said to "come, follow Me." It
made us purge a ton of things and helped us simplify
our lifestyle. It's been so healthy for us, as we learn
to trust in Him for our provision and be content
with where He has us financially. We continue to see
blessings in our life because of this change. Not necessarily monetarily, but spiritually, relationally, and
missionally, through the growth of our faith, through
the cultivation of new relationships this adventure
has brought us, and through a new mission in life we
wouldn't have known if we hadn't answered the call
and believed in the promise that it would be worth it
as long as we continue to follow Him.

* * *

I need to talk about one more thing that's running rampant
in Christian culture. There's a health, wealth, and prosper-
ity gospel that doesn't sit well with me. I believe God allows

suffering in our life sometimes (yes, even financial suffering) for us to see how much we need Him. He says, "In this world you will have trouble" (John 16:33). It's not to say you *might* have trouble; you will. Even as believers, suffering is still inevitable. In fact, you may suffer more for doing good: "Remember, it is better to suffer for doing good, if that is what God wants" (1 Peter 3:17).

But God also promises us abundant life here on earth, right now. He promises gifts to us—spiritual gifts of peace, joy, patience, love, and self-control. He promises that when we lose our life, we will find Him. When we give up our greed, our worldly desires, our pride, we will experience a more fulfilling life. "In this world you will have trouble. But take heart! I have overcome the world" (John 16:33).

With the condition my heart was in when I was fresh out of college and beginning my career path, it was in God's mercy that I didn't become financially successful, because it would have done greater harm than good to me and my character. Not only that, but my insatiable desire to become wealthy impacted my closest relationships, some of which never were fully repaired.

Regardless, it was used for my good: failure brought about the success of my character.

God knew the negative effects the success of this business would bring to my character...was already bringing to my character. Which is why, I believe, He withheld financial success—for good reason. Looking back, I'm thankful God allowed me to fail in this business, as it would have negatively impacted me more by succeeding than failure did. It would have added more fire to my already struggling pride-filled character, marked with greed.

There's a Biblical character with a similar and far more dramatic story than mine. We share so many resemblances I've often wondered if we were twins separated at birth...well, a few thousand years apart. It's the story of Joseph in the first book of Genesis. The story begins when Joseph was a young man, only seventeen. He got caught up in the shinier parts of what God revealed to him in a vision about his future. Joseph was a bit blinded by his own pride and had a sense of greed for making a great name for himself. He seemed to be a bit too excited about the fame of his future and the prospect of his brothers bowing down to him. Aren't most teenagers at seventeen a bit self-centered and prideful? Or perhaps his ego was a bit too elevated because his father doted on him—he was clearly the family favorite—making it difficult for him to see past his own arrogance? Even if his words were well intentioned, they were not well received. I wonder if he was even aware of his pride and the greedy nature of his statements.

As a side note, it may not always be wise to share your dreams with others, especially when jealousy and bitterness are there. Even if it's true and you believe God gave you this dream, it can come off as prideful if you aren't careful—especially if you share it with those who may already be jealous of you. Pray about it. Then ask yourself, *What's my motive in sharing this dream? Is it to get attention? Is it to make myself look better?* Or is your heart's desire to inspire others with this dream? Does sharing this dream provide a benefit to those around you? If not, it may be best to keep it to yourself, at least for now.

Whether unintentional or not, Joseph's prideful gloating about his vision of greatness cast a severe relational wedge between him and his already jealous brothers. His lack of sensitivity and inability to see his great vision from their point of view created a domino effect of negative events in his life for the next decade—he was nearly killed by his own brothers, sold as a slave, and thrown into jail. But perhaps this was God's plan all along.

God knew Joseph needed refining. It led to a difficult twelve-year journey filled with unexpected twists and turns, and extreme hardships that peeled away his pride layer by layer.

But, through all the trials and hardships, God was with him! Because Joseph trusted God and continued to seek an intimate relationship with Him, Joseph's character was transformed.

In summary, Joseph became second in command to the king of Egypt, the wealthiest in the country. He ruled with authority after experiencing a decade of hardship and severe poverty. And because of his significant seat of authority, and his ability to listen to God's instructions, he was able to store up food for the nation before the famine hit—as God told him it would.

This famine propelled his starving and struggling family to come before him asking for help. But this is the most beautiful and awe-inspiring part! When reunited with his family, instead of despising his brothers for throwing him in a pit and then selling him as a slave, Joseph showed them mercy and forgiveness! Joseph's heart was truly changed from one of pride and greed to one of generosity and humility. He extended forgiveness, which I don't think would have been possible if he were still that prideful boy of seventeen. It would have ended very differently if he had demanded that his brothers bow to him—nullifying any hope of relational repair—which seemed the more likely story at first. Instead, Joseph shared with his brothers that though their actions were meant for evil, God used them for His greater purpose—to save the nation from starvation. Not only that, but God also reunited Joseph's family, healing and restoring their broken relationships through Joseph's humble submission to extend forgiveness to his brothers. His dream really did come true—better than expected. What a surprise gift!

* * *

Although my network marketing career didn't pan out (thankfully), I now see how God had a better and healthier plan for me: to inspire and help women follow Jesus through this ministry of writing and speaking. And I've been able to experience humility in a tangible way. God, in His mercy, has blessed my husband and me financially more than I thought possible, though at the time of this writing, our bank account is at its lowest, and our income is drastically less than it was before. We are giving more generously and generating less money, and yet it feels completely right. I don't say any of this to gloat, but to give you hope and a glimpse into the reality that you too can change; your heart can become freed from the incessant desire for more wealth. I've come to realize that money is just money—it's simply another tool given to us to steward for God's glory.

* * *

Are you experiencing failure in your business, relationships, or another area of your life? Is it possible God is withholding something from you or allowing you to experience failure to bring about something better? Perhaps God is bringing you through a stressful situation in your finances to reveal a part of your character that needs pruning. Perhaps God has an even better plan for you in your struggle through joblessness, singleness, barrenness, lifelessness—but you just don't see it yet.

Sometimes you just don't see all that God is doing until later in the journey. This has been my experience so often. God's purposes aren't usually revealed until you look back to see how God redeemed that failed situation for His good and His glory.

God cares more about enhancing your character than extending your comfort. He wants to refine or strip away the subtle sin of worshipping money, stuff, and titles that is holding you back from becoming who you are meant to be. That means He will allow failures and hard situations to occur in order to bring about more good in your character.

Place your trust in Him. He is trustworthy, despite what you may believe at this time, because with Him by your side, all things *will* work out for the good of those who love and follow Him still (Romans 8:28).

Borrow This Refining Prayer When Words Are Few

LORD, reveal to me areas of struggle and idol worship that I have about money. Where I have issues with pride or selfish ambitions to build up my own earthly kingdom. I confess that my thoughts and actions about money, stuff, and status aren't always healthy and are hindering a deeper relationship with You. Help me remember that nothing else truly matters except stewarding what we've been given to help us grow Your eternal Kingdom. Help me put my true love toward You instead of the things of this world. In Jesus's name, amen.

CHAPTER 6

Body Wars

The first time I ever threw up my food on purpose after eating was in college. It wasn't a regular thing, but I did this occasionally if I really splurged. Internally, I knew this was a disordered way of eating, which was why I didn't do it often. But I also didn't think it was a big problem.

In college I also obsessed over how much I ate, or should I say, how little. I wasn't anorexic, but I did have a calorie-counting obsession, making sure I didn't eat more than 1,200 calories per day to keep my petite five-foot, two-inch frame nice and slim. I stayed just above the underweight mark for my height, so I wouldn't cross that sinful line—whatever that line was. I exercised at least an hour or more a day, less for health reasons and more because I coveted the way my body looked.

I didn't consider any of this a problem. I was hovering on that magic sin line—not quite across it but just before it was a *real* problem. A line, it seems, we all create in our minds to make us feel better about being only a little wrong. Just halfway sinful, not full blown. Or so I thought.

Proud of the fact that I wasn't "that girl" with a major eating disorder, I wasn't aware how much disordered eating was distorting my mind and my relationship with God.

It wasn't until I listened closely to what my mind was really telling me that I realized I wasn't as free from the issue as I'd thought. The truth is, while I was obsessing over making sure my body was in shape, my mind was severely out of shape. I was shackled by negative thinking and self-controlled mechanisms about how I wanted my body to look, never feeling fully satisfied. It wasn't until I finally got honest with myself a decade later, sitting down with a counselor, that I saw the weight of my sin.

* * *

Looking back, I wish I had been kinder to myself when I was "in my prime." Things have drastically changed with my body since having three children in less than two years.

For the record, I had no idea the toll a twin pregnancy would take on my body. While many of my friends had cute, round baby bellies all throughout their pregnancies with no complications, I was quickly nicknamed "Torpedo Belly" when not one but two babies crowded my insides. It wreaked havoc on my six-pack abs, as I rapidly became larger than most pregnant mamas. I also had a rare complication that affects fewer than 1 percent of all pregnant women, in which my body created more amniotic fluid than normal. Instead of measuring like a normal twin pregnancy, my belly measured like I was carrying triplets. Oh, the joy.

The same complication occurred in my second pregnancy (only eleven months later, mind you), carrying just one baby this time. However, you'd think one less baby would make things better.

Toward the last few months I was in excruciating pain as the buildup of fluid and the growing baby ripped my stomach muscles and the inner layers of my torso. I lay on the exam table while my doctor took out her special pregnancy measuring tape, wrapping it around my belly. "You're carrying like triplets, with just one!" she exclaimed.

That was truly a low moment for me. At the same time, I finally felt justified in never, ever wanting to be pregnant again. I'm pretty sure I have post-traumatic stress from being pregnant. Is that a thing?

Everywhere I went, others would stare at me like I was Octomom. The best comment was by a nurse on the day of my C-section with my daughter (one baby, remember, not two): "How many babies do you have in there?" she asked, wide-eyed.

I half smiled, wanting to punch her flat, tiny gut. Mumbling through gritted teeth, I managed to say, "There's just one."

"No way!" I could see it in her face that she didn't believe me.

While I'm super thankful my babies were born healthy and they made it out of their high-risk environment without side effects, I need to be real with you: I struggle deeply with how my body looks now in the aftermath.

Some women bounce back and look exactly like they did before. In fact, I've had to delete a few friends on Instagram because their post-baby bodies kill me with envy and jealousy. You too? Or maybe you're a bit like me as you sit there right now looking down at your jelly-like belly, relearning to ~~love~~ like it again. That may even be a stretch for you. Tolerate. Yes, that's more like it.

Or maybe it's not your belly but it's the flab on your arms. Or how thick your thighs are and how they rub together. Or maybe you have the opposite issue and can't keep weight on. Maybe your acne is atrocious, your teeth are terrible, or your hair says "hallelujah" all the time, refusing to be tamed.

For years, I prided myself on my toned stomach. Now, no matter how many sit-ups and planks I do, my stomach just isn't bouncing back like Britney Spears's. The reality is, Britney probably had a little nip and tuck after having her kids, which hardly any of us can afford. Even with cosmetic surgery, it doesn't always look the way you'd hoped.

I can say this personally, because I went through it.

After two very abnormal pregnancies (with three beautiful kids to show for it), stretching my belly to a degree most never have to experience, I had severe loss of muscle tension and structure in my stomach. They've given a name to this type of condition. It's called diastasis. Basically, it involves a permanent separation of my stomach muscles. Because of this, my back went out on me constantly due to lack of muscle strength, not to mention I had a permanently protruding belly that looked as if I were five months pregnant all the time. Literally. Surgery was highly recommended.

Then my gynecologist noticed my protruding belly button. "Has your belly button always looked like this?" she asked politely.

Ugh, no, lady. Can't you tell my belly and its button look like they went through the meat grinder?

I learned another term that day: umbilical hernia. More joy.

Apparently having an umbilical hernia isn't a joyful matter, though. It can lead to life-threatening side effects, which she mentioned, and I confirmed with Google (of course).

So apparently, I had clinical issues pointing me to surgery—which made me feel a little better about getting some work done to get my belly back to a more pleasant-looking shape again.

I also noticed one other thing I struggled with about my body that I never struggled with before. After milking two babies at the same time, my boobs just didn't look like, well, boobs anymore. In fact, one went completely flat (no joke) while the other became a saggy semblance of a B-plus. Bras were irritating because I no longer knew which size to choose! *Do I help my left side or my right side out?* One was either falling out of the cup or one wasn't filling up the cup, depending on my decision. Both were rightly annoying.

Honestly, until this moment, I had never considered having breast surgery.

Before I go much further, I need to address something. There are some of you who have had breast surgery and others of you who are appalled by my even talking about this. Some of you think it's a sin, while others of you say it isn't. Some of you think getting them done is warranted if you have had breast cancer and a mastectomy, while others of you say, "You need to love what God gave you."

This is one of those gray lines for me. There's no direct Scripture supporting or negating breast surgery. It doesn't say if it's right or wrong. Therefore, you must read between the lines of Scripture. Where I see it boil down is this: it is always a matter of the heart and whether or not we're contented. We must do an honest heart check for our motives. "For where your treasure is, there your heart will be also. 'The eye is the lamp of the body. So, if your eye is healthy, your whole body will be full of light, but if your eye is bad, your whole body will be full of darkness. If then the light in you is darkness, how great is the darkness!'" (Matt. 6:21–23, ESV).

Where is your treasure? Is it in your looks? Will you be content only when your body looks a certain way? If your body stays the same and doesn't change, can you learn to love it and be content with what you have?

How do you perceive yourself? Do you see yourself the way God sees you? Is it full of God's light, truth, and purpose or is it filled with bitterness, jealousy, and discontentment?

I had to go through some serious heart-to-hearts with myself over this decision to go through surgery. Was it godly? Could I be content without it? Could I justify it? There were medical conditions pointing me toward having it. At least for the stomach. But what about the breasts? Was this *really* necessary? Was I doing it because of societal pressure—what we should desire our bodies to look like?

After a lot of prayer and soul-searching, and conversations with my husband (who, by the way, loves me no matter what my body looks like), I decided to go ahead with it. My heart felt in the right place about it, and I needed to undergo surgery anyway.

However, God revealed certain discontents I didn't realize were still there.

Four years post-surgery, I can honestly say that although it functions better than it used to, and my bras fit nicely now, and my back isn't going out on me nearly as much, I'm still not fully satisfied with my body. I still didn't overcome my struggle with the way my body looks. I'm still aching over the fact that my belly was so severely damaged that it will never be the same again, even with surgery.

Expectations left me a bit unfulfilled to say the least. I've cried about it. Mourned it. And I heard God whisper, *What are you seeking? Satisfaction through your body? Contentment for the way you look? Don't you know I love you and that you are beautiful no matter what you look like? Can you love yourself no matter how imperfect you look?*

I want to say I'm that godly Christian woman who doesn't struggle with this issue anymore. I want to say that I've fully overcome feeling dissatisfied about the way my body looks. But I can't. I've had to mourn what will never be again, to accept my body, scars and all. I've had to embrace God like never before in this season where I'm only growing older and it is becoming impossible to eat a half gallon of ice cream like I did as a teen without adding pounds to my posture. But through this acknowledgment and admission, through the mourning of what feels hopeless and lost, I'm discovering a subtle settling in my heart: more moments of contentment about my form as I turn to Him; more glimpses of seeing myself the way God sees me: beautiful, adored, perfectly loved.

Friend, I give you permission to mourn what you once had or what never will be with your body. You need to mourn, shed some tears, cry out in frustration, and admit that you are struggling with your looks. Don't hide from it, because God already knows your heart. He hears your pain. He sees you scrutinizing yourself every time you walk by the mirror. He sees your sin and the discontentment you feel, but He doesn't shame you for it. He wants you to be open and real about it because that is when true healing comes. That's when you are more able to fully focus on Him, which enables you to start seeing yourself the way He sees you. You need to let go of what once was and embrace the new you with all your flaws and frustrations, because until you do, you'll never find contentment and satisfaction with yourself. You will continue to distance yourself from God's love (and others) because you'll be seeking contentment and love elsewhere, forgetting that God loves you with a true, never-ending love.

This is the sin of our hearts: forgetting that God loves us—forgetting that He loves us without a measuring stick.

And now you need to stand in front of a mirror and add this battle cry to your life: "I am not unlovable because of my size. I am not unsightly because of my scars. I am God's chosen, adored daughter created in His image, for a beautiful purpose." Keep telling yourself this until you start to believe it. When you start to believe it, that's when your true beauty will be released. A confidence and glowing radiance that comes only from God Himself. Because God don't make no junk. Beauty is in the eye of the beholder. And God beholds your beauty, no matter how many scars and stretch marks your body has.

We need to exercise to be healthy, but stop excessive exercise if we're seeking internal contentment from external gains. We need to eat healthily, but stop obsessively counting calories and start counting our blessings: my arms may be large, but they allow me to hold my babies; my belly may be bouncy, but it's a great pillow for my kids' heads to lie on; my thighs may be thick, but they are attached to strong legs that take me from point A to point B.

We need to be active to be healthy, choose self-care instead of self-obsession, watch what we consume to have the right energy we need. We do these things because it makes us strong women of God, enabling us to do the work God has called us to do, not because we are seeking a certain standard for our body to fit into.

There's one more thing that's inevitable that we all must face. To not recognize and embrace this may trigger another tailspin with your struggle.

* * *

Only a few years ago, in my early thirties, I noticed something new. Getting closer to the mirror and working to relax my face, I couldn't get away from it anymore. They were there to stay.

Smile lines. Also known as eye wrinkles.

Well, shoot. I wasn't particularly excited about this, but I had to succumb to the truth: I'm aging.

However, aging isn't celebrated in our current American culture. Many cultures around the world don't see this as a good thing either. Everywhere we look, ads are bombarding us about another cream for cellulite and wrap for wrinkles. We are forced to believe that our natural bodies and the natural aging process aren't just bad, they are unacceptable. In fact, aging is dreaded.

It wasn't until I was sitting in a dermatologist's office a few years ago to treat my adult acne (another insecurity I've had to deal with) that someone else pointed out this unacceptable truth. "You want me to take care of those wrinkles around your eyes?" the doctor asked with a smug smirk.

A little shocked by his bold statement (I guess I should expect this living in image-driven Southern California), I acted like I didn't know what he meant. "By doing what exactly?" I asked.

"Just a few injections of Botox should do the trick with those wrinkles around your eyes," he said cheerily.

In the bathroom mirror that night I found myself scrutinizing every wrinkle on my face, suddenly saddened by the reality of my fading youth—confirmed once again (by a doctor, no less) that this was unacceptable.

Maybe you're noticing the slowdown of your metabolism, the chronic aches and pains of your body, or a first gray hair.

Maybe you have chronic acne at the age of forty and you're continually bombarded by skincare consultants whenever you walk by their booths. They remind you that your acne is only acceptable for an adolescent and can be covered up with their expensive, heavy makeup, which they claim won't create more pimples even though your skin would be matted down with clay-like powder.

Maybe you have a slightly crooked nose, a chipped tooth, too many freckles, or cracked cuticles that someone points out from time to time, tugging again on your insecurity tank.

Maybe you have permanent damage to your face and body due to a major accident because of which your body (and brain) will literally never be the same again, and others stare at you at best or make you feel ugly and inhuman at worst.

What if your body never looks the way you want it to? What if no matter how many crunches you pursue or how much Botox you apply, it doesn't satisfy? What if you completely exhaust yourself (and your finances) in order to look a certain way, only for it to last so long? What if aging were celebrated instead of dreaded in our culture? Wouldn't that be amazing?

Friend, the truth is that our bodies are meant to grow old.

They are meant to wrinkle, get lumpy, and even a little saggy. It's inevitable. And while this may be a painful reality for you, you must learn to embrace it, accept it, and love yourself through it to become free from your vanity struggles.

I'm learning to love my ever-growing and changing body. I'm learning to love my smile lines, the lost luster of my skin tone, and accept some of the changes I cannot prevent. I'm learning to pursue health not for the way my body looks but for the energy it creates in me. I'm learning that my importance does not come from my fading appearance, but from the unchanging significance that I'm given by being a daughter of the King. I'm learning to lean into the struggle instead of pretend I don't, because it reminds me to turn my eyes back toward the Creator who created me. I remember to recite His truths over and over again:

- "Draw near to God, and he will draw near to you" (James 4:8).
- "For we are God's handiwork, created in Christ Jesus to do good works, which God prepared in advance for us to do" (Eph. 2:10).
- "I praise you because I am fearfully and wonderfully made; your works are wonderful, I know that full well" (Psalm 139:14).
- "The mind governed by the flesh is death, but the mind governed by the Spirit is life and peace" (Romans 8:6).

Choose to go to these often and believe in the truths of God's Word so that your mind dwells daily on the life and peace of God.

MIND WARS

If you had told me a few years ago that the way I thought about myself would affect my relationship and intimacy with God, I probably would have smiled politely while thinking, *Girl, every woman struggles with this issue . . . It's normal. And there's no cure. Move on.*

It's inevitable, right? This struggle? I'm sure there are a select few of you who are reading this chapter right now and don't really struggle with this. You're like, "Let's move on." But, for what I believe is true of 99 percent of the female population, we *all* struggle with this at some point in our lives, or perhaps (like me) throughout the majority of our lives.

Some people say, "Well, the cure to this is simply to stop thinking those negative thoughts!" Believe me, I wish there were a delete button for negative thinking, so I didn't have to struggle with this ever again.

So what do we do? What's the solution to this chronic issue? We can't completely stop these negative thoughts from coming, but we can *redirect* them.

Every time I hear that negative voice whisper to me . . .

You're so fat.

Your skin is so ugly.

Your beauty is lacking.

I redirect those lies to remember the truth from my Creator . . .

You are beautiful no matter what size you are. "You formed my innermost parts; You knit me together in my mother's womb" (Psalm 139:13, AMP).

Your external beauty doesn't define who you are. "Charm is deceitful, and beauty is vain, but a woman who fears the LORD is to be praised" (Prov. 31:30).

You're beautiful, even as you age. "Though our outer self is wasting away, our inner self is being renewed day by day" (2 Cor. 4:16).

God doesn't promise us that we won't struggle. He doesn't promise that the enemy will stop its whispers in our ear. But He does promise to give us another way around it. While the thoughts may arise, we don't have to succumb to them. Acknowledge them (don't pretend they're not there), then redirect them to the refining truth and restore your heart again.

The tricky part is, this isn't a "one time and you've overcome" process. It's a continual process to fight daily for the freedom that is already yours! If you don't put up a fight, this destructive mind-set will overcome your heart, mind, and soul in damaging ways.

You need to know: no matter what size you are, what color your skin is, how many wrinkles you have, how many stretch marks lace your belly, how big or small your nose or forehead is, how saggy your breasts are, or the number on the scale…you are created in the image of God. He didn't mess up making you. You are not a mistake. You are not ugly. You are His beautiful masterpiece, and your worth is not based on any sort of measuring stick created by people. You don't need an app filter to re-create you. God has already created you, and His beauty skills are far better than an app filter. Even though you may struggle with all your dieting, binging, minimal eating, exercising, hair-coloring, Botoxing, nip-and-tucking, remember *He still loves you.* But just so you know, all the dieting, binging, minimal eating, exercising, hair-coloring, Botoxing, excessive exercising and nip-and-tucking will never be enough until you release the insatiable desire to look a certain way, different from how you currently are, right now.

So give it to Him, girlfriend. Let Him refine away the lies that you're ugly, unlovable, and unworthy. Let's stand together and embrace the woman in the reflection, accept her for who she is right now, and try on the wardrobe of His truth that gives us freedom to live wholly with a contagious confidence that comes from Him alone.

Borrow This Refining Prayer When Words Are Few

Abba Father, help me see myself the way You see me: beautiful, significant, and lovely in every way. I'm sorry I have forgotten Your truths about this. I'm sorry I haven't taken as much intentional effort to strip away this lie that plagues my thoughts. I confess this to You now and ask that You help me turn my eyes to Your truth every time I feel myself scrutinizing my appearance in a negative way. I am choosing now to live confidently and contently in who I am, not in who I wish I was or desire to look like. Thank You for revealing to me this truth. In Jesus's name, amen.

CHAPTER 7

Love and Lust

It seemed so harmless. The occasional flirtatious word. A hand on the back.

Soon I found myself on a lifeguard tower, long after sundown, intertwining hands with a man I'd just met at my new job. The butterflies in my belly were fluttering with excitement, something I hadn't felt for a while. Silky words tumbled out of his lips, captivating my attention and wooing my dry, brittle heart.

No big deal, right?

A ring glistened on my finger, reminding me of my vows only fifteen months prior to a man who wasn't the man standing in front of me. No, *that* man was home, safely unaware of his wife's predicament and current betrayal.

I shouldn't be doing this. Oh, God, I shouldn't be doing this!

As he got closer, I noticed his smell. Much to my surprise, I crinkled my nose. There was a sway in his steps.

One of many alarms started ringing through my head that this entire situation was a bad idea.

He was intoxicated.

I turned away and tried to focus on the dark, rolling waves just beyond where we were standing. As I leaned against the railing, my thoughts churned and swung violently back and forth from one emotion to the next.

A full moon encircled us in unsettling light, as if it knew what we were doing and the pivotal, life-changing decision I was about to make. Tinkling wineglasses echoed toward us from the beach bar where our co-workers were enjoying themselves.

I felt this man wrap his arms around my waist. He nuzzled my neck...

What am I doing? Waves of guilt, shame, and dread churned inside me. I hated what I was doing. I knew it was wrong. And yet, I felt completely and utterly rooted to this spot. Why was I not running from this? Why was I still here?

"I can't do this..." I mumbled, hoping he would stop what I couldn't seem to stop myself.

He paused.

"You are so beautiful," he slurred. "And I really want to kiss you..."

As I glanced up at the dark of the night, my insides screamed. My flesh wanted to follow desire. My heart was torn. My soul knew this was not what I *really* wanted. Unable to do anything else, I prayed a silent prayer...

Lord, help me.

Three simple words. An honest plea to find strength I didn't have. A strength beyond my flesh to overcome the infatuating desire for this man that I knew would destroy my life, my marriage, and my future.

I didn't want this. Not really.

He had none of the amazing qualities my husband possessed.

My husband—who wrote letters to me every week during our college summers apart. Yes, back when snail mail was a thing and texting wasn't quite as popular as it is now. My husband—who hand-carved a wooden box with roses detailing the top and inside, one hundred Hershey's kiss wrappers with his writing of all the reasons he loved me. My husband—who stood between me and my family when they shamed me for walking away from the Mormon faith. My husband—who jokes and smiles about everything, wraps me in his broad shoulders when I'm feeling down, and has a depth and knowledge of the Bible that puts scholars to shame.

However, in recent months we had felt increasingly disconnected and distracted, mainly due to a depression I was starting to come out of. But this didn't give me permission to betray him with another man.

I had made a vow to him. I made a covenant with God: till death do us part.

Why then was I considering following the seductions of this other man? What was so alluring about him?

He *was* cute. Those deep eyes and dashing smile captivated me the first time I met him at work. But the part that grabbed me like a fish on a string was hearing those words: "You're so beautiful," "How are you so gorgeous?" "I wish you were single," "Why do you have to be so cool?"

He praised me in every way.

And quite frankly, I hadn't been receiving much from my husband lately. You see, my husband has a weakness when it comes to words. He doesn't say a lot. And his weakness is my greatest need.

The Five Love Languages, by Gary Chapman, talks about how we have five ways of communicating with one another: touch, quality time, gifts, acts of service, and words of affirmation.

Words of affirmation—this is my predominant love language.

Unfortunately, when my husband took this test, he scored lowest in this category. Combine his weakness with the depression I was experiencing (making it harder on my husband to find the right words to say), and my love tank was currently running on fumes.

Until I met *him*, the guy at work. He was speaking the words my heart was desperate to hear.

Therefore, as much as I didn't want to admit it, a spark had arisen, and I allowed a fire to grow. That fire was now raging out of control.

I felt his hand stroking my hair. My heart continued to melt.

Lord, please help me!

I turned and looked at this man before me. His eyes were full of passionate desire for me. But then...I noticed a flicker of something else. Something unnerving. What was it?

I searched his eyes with a steadier focus.

Oh!

There was something murky in them. Something utterly terrifying.

As he came toward me, his mouth puckered...and like a flash of light I saw the truth. His desire was drenched in fleeting, unholy lust...not the unending, pure love given to me freely by the man I married.

At that moment I knew the truth...and with strength beyond my own, I turned away from his kiss.

* * *

What happened next, I can't recall completely. But I remember feeling an energy inside me other than my own bravely telling him no as I quickly made my way off that lifeguard tower and away from him. I remember driving home to the man I had promised my heart and life to, a man I'm proud and thankful to say I've been married to for thirteen years as of September 2019.

Maybe you ended up with a different story and a different ending? Maybe you didn't walk away when you knew you should have, and things didn't work out as well for you as you hoped? Maybe you feel like your affair was justified? Maybe *you've* been the one cheated on? Or maybe you have only thought it, but never fully acted on it?

I don't know your story. I don't know whether you've

been holding on to guilt, shame, unforgiveness, or pain that's been burdening your heart for three days or thirty years. But I do know God wants to rewrite our broken stories to be used for His glory, no matter how sinful they are.

The only way we can remove the power of guilt, shame, unforgiveness, or pain is to share this burden with our Ultimate Bridegroom, to confess our unholiness before Him.

By not doing so, we miss out on the deeper intimacy and healing we can have with Jesus.

What if the healing and intimacy we are so desperate for is just within reach, but in our pride and unwillingness to surrender it all before God we miss it? What if the crippling weight of our sin—such as lust—is because we simply don't know how to get ourselves to say, "I'm sorry, Lord," or "Forgive me, Jesus," and accept the unconditional grace that's readily available to us?

What if our broken relationships could have been prevented if someone told us not to play with fire, because it's outside of God's beautiful design for marriage? I think there'd be a lot less brokenness and a lot more openness to understanding God's design for healthy sexuality.

WHAT *IS* GOD'S DESIGN FOR SEXUALITY?

In the beginning, there was a time and place when sin was absent from this world. It's a world we've never experienced, but it's what our hearts long for. Perfect intimacy. Perfect love. Perfect sex. Well, I don't know about the perfect sex part. But God created a man in His image named Adam. And through this man, God created a woman named Eve. God loved them both equally. "God blessed them and said, 'Be fruitful and multiply'" (Genesis 1:28, NLT). This was stated before sin entered the world. So perhaps the perfect sex part isn't too far off?

Sex is not wrong or sinful in its original form. And therefore, our sexuality is not a terrible thing, as some may think it is. God saw all that He created at the time of Adam and Eve's union and said, "It is good." The world was perfect. Adam and Eve were created for each other. Husband and wife, formed in such a way that they fit perfectly like puzzle pieces when they came together physically.

Friend, this is not a coincidence.

God created us physically to come together with our husband in a sensual, intimate way. He created us to form a covenant and bond as husband and wife, and then enjoy the sexual benefits that go with it. Unfortunately, once sin entered the picture, this design became tainted and used improperly. Lust, sexual immorality, adultery, and coveting became common. Sex outside of marriage has become normal in our culture. I won't even go into the deeper and darker parts of how God's design for sexuality has been abused because I think you know what those are.

However, these negatives surrounding our sexuality have our full attention these days. We have forgotten that sex is a good and holy act of intimacy in the context of God's design for husband and wife.

So, yes, sex is good in the context of marriage. Sex is

a beautiful, intoxicating act between husband and wife. If you don't believe that God loves sex, just turn to the Song of Songs in the Bible and prepare to blush with the erotic, poetic language it uses to describe a lovemaking experience between a newly married husband and wife.

So what's my point?

We need to understand the origin of sexuality—that God meant it for good, in the context of marriage between a man and woman—before we continue to move into revealing the subtle sin areas that we women struggle with when it comes to our sexuality. We also need to understand that while there is a physical side to this union, there are also spiritual forces surrounding this powerful connection.

THE UNSEEN FORCES

There's a distinct but subtle shift that occurs when we speak our vows to the person we commit to be with forever. And I'm not talking about having sex. I'm talking about the unseen spiritual forces that are vehemently against your relationship and seeking to wreak havoc on you.

Here is a radical and powerful realization that nobody talks about: before marriage, Satan is trying to get you into bed with your boyfriend. The moment you say, "I do," Satan is trying to get you out of bed with your husband.

God loves your purity before marriage. And if God loves purity before marriage, then it means the enemy of God is working against what's pure and holy—he wants you to engage in sexual acts before marriage.

God loves marriage and wants it to remain pure. And if God loves marriage, then it means the enemy of God is working against what's pure and holy—he is working to eliminate intimacy through sex between a husband and wife.

Unfortunately, we have turned a blind eye to the enemy and his manipulations as he seeks to coerce us into these unholy acts. We start to commingle with the enemy by allowing our boyfriend to take us to second and third base, feeling justified enough because we aren't going for the full home run. Or we allow that engagement ring to decide for us, *What the heck!* and proceed to give ourselves over to our fiancé before saying, "I do."

What we fail to realize is that the sinful offenses we shrug off set us and our relationship with the other person up for potential disaster. We like to say, "It's no big deal!" Until one day, it *is* a big deal—like an unwanted pregnancy, a one-night stand, or a hollowed-out soul from engaging in this beautiful act in the wrong way. You cry out in despair from the pain of it all, wishing it had never happened in the first place.

Perhaps nobody has told you these subtle infractions give the enemy increasing power and leverage over your mind, body, and soul. Perhaps you don't realize how sneaky the enemy is—a thief seeking to steal, kill, and destroy your life, propelling you into deeper destruction . . . one seemingly insignificant step at a time.

When I was on that lifeguard tower with the other man, allowing an emotional affair (and nearly a physical one) to take place, it wasn't because I saw this man randomly walking down the street and thought, *Hey, let's hook up!*

First, we spent a lot of our working hours together. We got to know each other, and he started to tell me things like, "Why do all the married girls have to be so beautiful?" and "Why do you have to be so cute?" Next, it was exchanging looks. Those lingering, penetrating gazes pulled at my insides in an exciting way. Those flirtatious words then became a gentle hand on my back as he consoled me or a compassionate squeeze of my hand. And if I had been single, well, this would be normal and totally appropriate. But I was married to another man, so it was wrong, right? I mean, you're not supposed to flirt with other men or engage in flirting back, correct? Or maybe you think it's not a big deal?

You may convince yourself it's harmless, but what is it doing to your heart? The enemy wants you to believe it's not a big deal, that the flirtatious looks, personal texts, or coffee together before work is all normal.

Girl, even if you firmly believe your heart is in the right place, what you are doing right now is playing with fire. And here's the thing about fire ... it's dangerous when you don't know how to play by the rules.

When you're single, this spark is what helps you find a possible suitor. It's a good thing! But when you're married, using this spark to create fire with anyone other than your spouse is playing outside God's rulebook.

The rules are there for our protection. It's not to take the fun out of it. God knows the power of sex, how it can cultivate such elating joy, soothing pleasure, and a deep bond between you and your spouse. It is breathtakingly beautiful and holy when used respectfully between a husband and wife. But when used in the wrong way, its power for good becomes a power for great destruction and brokenness in one's life.

Let me tell you the honest truth: there will be men other than your husband who cause that unsuspecting "spark" in your heart. It's that sudden tug that you feel deep down, a strong connection, that says this certain someone has something that you like. For whatever reason, they have character qualities or a perfectly chiseled body (*ahem*) that creates a spark of interest, which is meant to lead to connection. But while you may feel that initial spark, it's deadly and sinful only if you provide the kindling. Without the kindling, the spark will go out and you will be left with harmless acknowledgment that it was there.

The real danger comes when you allow that spark in your heart become the kindling for something more, smoldering into a steady, warm, intoxicating fire. At first you say, "It's no big deal," because the fire is small and can easily be put out with a brief blast of a fire extinguisher. But what you don't know is that these flirtatious fires grow rapidly as soon as you turn a blind eye to their lustful flames.

Those subtle texts turn to more fantasy-filled thoughts, which turn to "Let's grab coffee," which turn to landing on a lifeguard tower and wondering what in the world happened! Lacking immediate action to stop the flame, that tiny spark soon rages into a wildfire. And we all know wildfires are extremely dangerous.

Maybe you still wonder how those seemingly insignificant sparks with this other man turned into a violent wildfire, causing so much pain, brokenness, and destruction. I did too, until the day I came across a passage of Scripture and realized it all starts with matters in the mind.

MIND MATTERS

"You're so beautiful..."

This is how it started.

I rolled those words around in the synapses of my brain over and over again.

He likes me!

I dwelled on this thought and enjoyed it! Especially the way his eyes sparkled at me when he said it. It felt good to feel attractive. And of course, I thought, *What does it hurt to enjoy the flirtation and fantasize over it all day?!* Oh, but it does.

Science attests to the fact that our mind plays a vital role in the development of our actions and how our life plays out. And then there's an ancient script that said this exact same thing more than two thousand years ago. "Carefully guard your thoughts because they are the source of true life" (Prov. 4:23, CEV).

Our mind plays a vital role when it comes to our actions.

What we think about is what comes about. Every choice we make comes from a few thousand neurons and synapses firing in our brain, directing our next move. So the more we dwell on whatever is it that we are dwelling on, the more likely these thoughts will become our actions.

As Lysa TerKeurst writes, "If we allow our thoughts to stink, that smell will leak out of every bit of us—our words, our actions, and especially our reactions."[1]

If you dwell on lustful thoughts about a man other than your husband, you are more likely to eventually make that fantasy a reality. If you are dwelling on lustful thoughts with your boyfriend before marriage, you're more likely to cross the line sexually too early and risk unfortunate consequences. Unless you take those thoughts captive to Christ.

This powerful passage of Scripture attests to the spiritual forces against us and how we can overcome them:

> *The weapons we fight with are not the weapons of the world. On the contrary, they have divine power to demolish strongholds. We demolish arguments and every pretension that sets itself up against the knowledge of God, and we take captive every thought to make it obedient to Christ. (2 Cor. 10:4–5)*

Maybe you are making excuses right now about how this subtle sin of dwelling on lustful thoughts really isn't a big deal. Maybe you haven't experienced firsthand your lustful thoughts toward someone else coming true. You've been dreaming of Brad Pitt in his underwear for years, and he hasn't shown up on your doorstep to make your thought fantasy a reality yet. It's quite possible you won't ever act on your thoughts and engage in inappropriate sexual relations with another, but does this mean enjoying these lustful thoughts is still okay?

We don't realize that enjoying this subtle sin prevents us from engaging in a deeper, more intimate relationship with Jesus, which is the whole heart of this book—to help you experience a more vibrant, fulfilling relationship with Jesus!

But you may be hindering it with subtle sexual sins you're not even aware of.

I never anticipated that the flirtatious words and advances toward me by this other man would turn into something more. I never anticipated that the lustful thoughts I had toward him would turn into an emotional affair and nearly into a physical one. I never knew that these thoughts prevented deeper intimacy and connection with God in a way that left me feeling like God had given up on me.

And, friend, I want to prevent you from going down the wrong path like I did when I allowed these unholy thoughts to run rampant, causing physical pain and emotional destruction, but, more importantly, spiritual reduction. I want you to refine away the lies that tell you those seemingly insignificant flirtations or dwelling on lustful thoughts aren't a big deal.

I pray that you turn your mind back to Scripture, as I did. Check your heart against His Word to decipher whether you're mentally engaging in something that is for God or against God. We must turn away from sin and turn toward God, because only then are we able to experience the intimacy with Christ once again that we are desperate to enjoy.

Here are some practical ways I've removed the negative, lustful thoughts (or prevented actions):

- *Pray and repent.* It sounds simple, but it's so powerful. It doesn't matter if your eyes are open or closed, if you're in a private room or a crowd full of people, God is always listening and ready to help. He has already forgiven you, but you must be the one to ask first.
- *Dwell on Scripture.* Memorize verses to help you dwell on the positive, holy things of God or give you the courage to turn away from sin. This verse is one of my favorites: "God is our refuge and strength, an ever-present help in trouble" (Psalm 46:1).
- *Phone a friend.* No joke! Make sure you have a close friend or two whom you can confide in and share your struggles with (or simply engage in conversation with) when you're faced with the temptation to dwell on lustful thoughts.
- *Think about having sex with your husband.* Seriously. If you're thinking sexual thoughts about someone else, stop, and start directing that in a healthy, more holy way—like dwelling on the man you're married to.
- *Listen to worship music with words.* If you start singing those words, you will have a hard time thinking about anything else except Jesus (which is obviously a good thing).

Thankfully, no matter what happens, redemption is always possible.

REDEMPTION

I didn't tell the full story to my husband that night when I came home from the lifeguard tower. But I couldn't *not* share anything (my conscience wouldn't allow that). So I shared about how there was this guy from work who had been flirtatious with me and tried to kiss me. But I didn't tell him that I relished hearing this man's affirming words about me because I missed hearing them from my husband. I didn't tell him I allowed another man's hands to hold mine and enjoyed the butterflies in my stomach, which I hadn't felt in a while. I didn't tell him how much I desired in that moment to go further with the other man because the fire felt warmer there.

Shame and sin do that. They make you hide, run away. They make you share just enough but not the whole story for fear of the consequences.

But God's truth says, "In him we have redemption through his blood, the forgiveness of sins, in accordance with the riches of God's grace" (Ephesians 1:7). He paved the way for us by literally pouring out His blood for us on the cross, out of love for us, so we can experience the cloak of His grace.

Our sin, whether mental or physical, is the same to God. Whether we commit an affair in our mind or commit an affair in action, both are sin. Neither one weighs more than the other in God's eyes. However, the consequences of our sin may be different and hold more weight or pain over us than the other. We may lose our marriage because of an affair. We may get pregnant out of wedlock. These are physical consequences of our sin that can be extremely painful to experience and acknowledge.

While mentally fantasizing about that other man may not result in a tangible consequence, it still results in a spiritual wedge, distancing you from experiencing a deeper, more intimate relationship with Jesus. If this doesn't seem like a big deal to you, I'm worried for your heart. I'm worried it may be hardened from the truth of God's word and His law, which is to "be holy for [God is] Holy" (1 Peter 1:16).

I once believed the lies that said my lustful and inappropriate sexual thoughts were no big deal. But remember, our thoughts become our actions. And our relationship with Jesus becomes less vibrant as we hold on to sin and pridefully believe that repentance is unnecessary.

Can you do something for me? I want to encourage you to surrender your sins before Jesus, right now, and acknowledge any of those lustful, sexual thoughts you've been dwelling on. Forgive yourself as He forgives you, completely and wholly. Ask Him to help you turn your thoughts back to Him whenever they go down the rabbit trail of sensual fantasies.

Years later, I came clean with my husband. It wasn't fun. There was shared brokenness. But we worked through it. We believe in God's Word that says, "Repent, then, and turn to God, so that your sins may be wiped out, that times of refreshing may come from the Lord" (Acts 3:19). I also love this one: "Though your sins are like scarlet, they shall be as white as snow" (Isaiah 1:18).

Not only did a full healing of my soul take place and was

deeper trust formed by admitting my sin to my husband (which led to great makeup sex, by the way, and deeper intimacy with him), but a weight was lifted that I didn't realize I'd been carrying all those years because of this seemingly insignificant lustful infraction. I continue to come to Jesus with my thoughts whenever they start to lead me astray. And I have found the power to overcome lustful temptations in my mind with the Holy Spirit working through me to keep my thoughts and actions pure.

God desires us to be holy as He is holy (1 Peter 1:16). This doesn't mean we are supposed to be perfect (that's impossible). It doesn't mean we are supposed to fake it (that's insensible). It means we are to submit our infractions to Him, so we can experience the redemptive cleansing God paid the ultimate price for us to have and become free from the weight and wedge these trespasses create in our relationship with Him. When we do this, it's almost like God is able to move in even closer to us, which enables us to experience a richer, more revitalizing connection with Him, transforming us to become even more like the women we are meant to be.

Borrow This Refining Prayer
When Words Are Few

Father God, I submit to You right now any impure thoughts or actions that I've had regarding lust or sexual desires that are not within the boundaries You've given me to experience love and connection with another man. Help me bring my thoughts captive to You, turning away from sexual sin, and experience a deeper connection with You as I seek to be holy as You are holy. I'm thankful for Your unconditional love and grace toward me, to see me as white as snow. Bring freedom to my path as I take new steps to keep my eyes, mind, and body pure. In Jesus's name, amen.

CHAPTER 8

Overwhelmed

My brain raced through images, words, and places—a swirling vortex of chaos that wouldn't settle. My body was racked with tension. Heart pounding. Neurons firing at gut-wrenching speed. Exhausted—mind, body, and soul—sleep wouldn't come. This was my norm. This was just part of my DNA: overwhelmed with anxiety.

Or was it?

My anxiety has always been puzzling. Life for me has been void of much trauma; I know that's rare these days. I was raised in a home where money wasn't an issue and food was never lacking. I often took fun family vacations. My parents—although they've struggled at times—are still happily married and desperately love me. They've dropped everything at times to come help me. Once, my mom traveled more than three hundred miles to care for my sick kids because the pneumonia plague clung to me like a leech.

I've never been abused or molested. Like most people,

I've experienced the loss of grandparents and some friends. Even so, stress and anxiety followed me like a shadow... but I never really knew it. Maybe I just didn't want to believe it. Either way, it wasn't until I hit my thirties— juggling work, marriage, three kids, trying to keep a social life amidst #allthethings (you know what I'm talking about?)—that stress and anxiety became overwhelming to the point I couldn't ignore them anymore.

I had health-related symptoms. Not knowing they had to do with anxiety at the time, I was sure a doomsday prognosis would be discovered. *It's got to be cancer!*

After multiple tests and everything coming back normal, I was both thankful and yet discouraged that I couldn't figure out the why of my health issues. So I began a different approach to figuring out my symptoms. Yep, you guessed it, I Googled it.

Be careful of Google, though. You can diagnose yourself as having every dreadful disease on the planet with just one sniffle. If I'm being honest, my husband had to save me from being carried away by Googleitis more than once.

However, Google helped me see a few things I'd never thought of before. As I researched, prayed, researched, searched Scripture, and researched some more, I finally had a *whoa* moment. *Could this really be what I've been struggling with my whole life?*

Testing my newfound discovery, I shared this thought with my husband. "So, I'm beginning to think that my physical symptoms are related to anxiety or stress."

He pondered for a moment. "Well, yeah, that makes sense."

"But it's been going on for a while now. That means I've been struggling with anxiety for a long time."

He laughed. "You didn't know that about yourself?"

Stunned, I said, "Um, no! Really? You mean...you've known and never told me?"

"Well, yeah. It's pretty darn obvious. I didn't think it was something that needed pointing out." Back to reading he went, as if this was common knowledge.

But his casual reaction completely dismantled my last shreds of denial and forced me to embrace the truth—*I struggle with anxiety*. It may sound like a small and obvious admission to you, but it was a major admission for me. It was also a necessary first step that propelled me on the path toward overcoming stress, worry, and anxiety.

* * *

I could have blamed my anxiety on having three children in less than two years. I could have blamed my anxiety on my husband—his laid-back character and lack of planning often redlined my planner tendencies. I could have blamed my stress on so many external details around me that cause me stress. And I would have missed the key to overcoming this battle.

The reality is that most of my stress and anxiety is fueled by internal issues—unconscious beliefs rooted deep within me. I had to accept the reality that most of the stress and anxiety were coming from me.

This may not make sense to you yet, but I ask that you

give me a chance to show you how anxiety is an internal issue. Which is a good thing! External issues are not always possible to change. However, we do have the ability to change our internal thinking, allowing us to be in a position to overcome stress and anxiety in our daily lives. We can reprogram our brains to remember what is true. "The purposes of a person's heart are deep waters, but one who has insight draws them out" (Prov. 20:5). Understanding the inner workings of our hearts is intentional work. To sort out the strands, find what they are connected to, and figure out what they all mean requires time, energy, and the will to engage.

And I've lost you . . . "I'm too tired for this! I'm already overwhelmed. This is too hard! I'm not up for this. Can I just take a pill and move on with my life?"

I get it. Really, I do. Our society has us all conditioned to expect a quick fix, and this soul-searching stuff sounds like anything but a quick fix. I've been there too: overwhelmed at knowing I needed to change and overwhelmed by my inability to change. Stuck. Lost. Paralyzed. Frantically racing yet going nowhere.

Let me speak plainly here: you are neither wrong nor right for taking a pill. You are no better or worse a person if you decide to take medicine to treat this issue. But I would advise caution since taking a pill may take the anxiety symptoms away for a time but leave the root of the problem unhealed. This has happened to me. Medicine can be an effective tool that is *part* of your solution, but it is not always *the* solution. To really heal, we need to figure out what the root cause of your anxiety is in the first place.

Also, for those thinking you simply need more faith to pray away your anxiety, praise God's grace if that works for you. But for me—and for many others—anxiety has little to do with a lack of faith in God and has all to do with lack of understanding yourself, the root issue, and God's character. My anxiety is very much one of "all things" that God has worked for my good and has been one of the greatest tools to deepen and widen my faith. Telling someone he or she simply needs more faith is not only unfair, but it's also untrue, and while well intentioned for sure, it does more harm than good to their character. So please don't.

As Christians, we aren't without struggles. We don't suddenly become free of committing sin, experiencing tragic circumstances, or allowed exceptions to struggles—such as anxiety. This would imply perfection, and, goodness, we are far from perfect. But the beautiful thing is that imperfections lead us to Jesus. They reveal and remind us of our desperate need for Him to help us overcome our battles. Having a personal relationship with God is crucial to overcoming the battles in your life that you're facing.

* * *

Being a Christian simply means you've accepted God's grace over your life and submit to His leadership. It means you believe that Jesus died on the cross, offering a sacrifice to free you from the weight and bondage of poor choices.

To put it bluntly, Jesus bridged the gap between life in heaven or life in hell, paving the way to restore you into intimate fellowship with Him. This decision to have an intimate relationship with Him gives you the title of Christian, and when that happens, a transformation takes place in your soul as the Spirit of God comes to live within you. You see, God's sacrifice isn't just a get-out-of-hell-free card; He is your guide, your mentor, your knight in shining armor. He fills your soul and develops an intimate relationship with you through prayer and by reading the Bible.

And this is where the real freedom is for you right now. Remember the truth I shared with you above, the truth that was, in truth, overwhelming? "The purposes of a person's heart are deep waters, but one who has insight draws them out" (Prov. 20:5). Understanding the inner workings of our heart is intentional work. To sort out the strands, find what they're connected to, and figure out what they all mean requires time, energy, and the will to engage. But this is where the secret is. You're not doing this work on your own. While it's true that some effort is required, you're not the one responsible to draw out the deep motives of your heart—that burden is on your Lord and Savior, and He is more than willing and able to shoulder it. All He asks is that you bring your two fish and five loaves. Let Him do the rest.

Just as a little girl goes to her daddy for help, we too must go to our Father in heaven for help. But unlike our earthly parents who make mistakes or fail in providing us with help when we need it most, we can trust our Father in heaven to always be there for us and provide the exact wisdom we need. God knows the inner workings of your heart. He's just waiting for you to put aside fear and trust in Him as He guides you toward healing and wholeness—in this case, freedom from anxiety.

I encourage you to pause and ask God for a soft heart, open mind, and motivation as you press deeper and unearth the inner workings of your soul.

This was *the* hardest part for me. Admitting my struggles made me feel broken, ashamed, unsteady—*why can't I pull myself together?* It felt terminal, unchangeable, and final; but this is exactly what the enemy wants you to think.

Your acknowledgment isn't to your detriment; it's to your benefit. "The LORD mocks the mockers but is gracious to the humble" (Prov. 3:34, NLT). Acknowledging your struggles brings the issues out of the dark into the light where healing will happen.

* * *

I became a certified life coach in stress management not because I was an expert at managing my stress, but because I was a complete stress case and I *had* to figure out a way to get a handle on this battle. So, thanks to my training, I want to share with you a bit of what I've learned when it comes to overcoming stress in your daily life.

Scientifically speaking, anxiety, worry, and stress are all related to our *fight-or-flight* response. This is a mechanism in our body that enables us to take action when we enter a stressful or perceived stressful situation.

This fight-or-flight response can be a good thing. It can make you act during crucial moments. If you're being assaulted, your child is in danger, or your boss asks you to come in on Saturday, you will want this mechanism activated pronto to either "get the heck out of there" or "fight back because your life depends on it!"

But it can also go a bit haywire in our bodies. If we're constantly stressed and we don't take proper measures to turn off the fight-or-flight response, then it becomes a mechanism that is constantly on in our bodies—increasing fatigue, generating less focused attention, and it can even spiral our moods into depression (anxiety-induced depression), or we can experience other unwanted psychological responses.

When we have deadlines at work, overwhelming responsibilities at home, or kids requiring our constant attention, underlying fears can be the cause of these stressful situations:

- We fear we won't meet our deadlines.
- We fear connecting with another person intimately.
- We fear sending our children off to school.
- We fear an economic crash in the future.

So we live in this constant state of fear, ready to fight or ready to take flight. What once was a good and healthy subconscious biological function changes from friend to foe. This constant state of anxiety makes us less productive, more exhausted, and physically and/or psychologically ill to the point of a complete breakdown (panic attack, anyone?). We get so overwhelmed with fear, we end up living stressed, anxious, and worried about every little thing. All. The. Time. This is not the way we were meant to live.

How can we overcome this? You're beginning to do it already! By becoming educated on what the underlying cause of stress and anxiety is—fear—you've taken the next step to become free from this issue.

Next, you need to understand what's going on in your body when you are in this stressed state. You need to understand how we internalize stress very differently from one person to the next, since there are varying types of stress.

* * *

Have you ever experienced a traumatic event? Psychologists claim traumatic events include death in the family, divorce, experiencing an affair, being sexually assaulted, and going to war. These events can cause a condition called post-traumatic stress disorder (PTSD)—a severe form of stress. Deeper intervention is often necessary to help one cope, such as PTSD counseling, anti-anxiety or depression medication (used temporarily), and other therapeutic measures with the goal of getting our bodies back to a normal state of function.

But what about the everyday stress? Work, school, managing finances, cultivating our marriage/relationships, or parenting are daily life stressors we all face to some degree. Some psychologists call it acute stress, which in turn can create chronic stress, depending on how we internalize and handle stress. Interestingly, psychologists say these daily stressors can be just as damaging and life-threatening as experiencing severe post-traumatic stress events, so this isn't something to take lightly.

I'm not going to highlight all the spectrums of stress; I'm simply going to focus more heavily on the everyday stressors we all face—especially since stress from traumatic events is best handled under the guidance of a licensed counselor—and help lead you toward taming that chronic stress into remission.

* * *

A quick recap of what you just learned: the mechanism of stress is a fight-or-flight response. Without going into too much detail, when we face a stressful situation (real or perceived), this triggers our bodies to simultaneously release certain hormones and chemicals that help us adapt or react to the stressful situation at hand. The problem with this mechanism comes when the switch short-circuits and is left on—permanently.

Think about it. If you leave a pot of boiling water on the stove, eventually the water will boil away, burning up the now-dry pot. Or maybe you left your coffeepot on all day, with no coffee in it, burning up the pot. Hard to do these days with those automatic off sensors, but you get the idea.

Do you see the resemblance? These days most electrical devices—computers, cell phones, coffeepots—turn off automatically when they've been running too long. They sense when it's time to rest! Do you?

Our minds and bodies are meant to have periods of rest. From sleep to spiritual meditation to some other form of stress relief, we need to have periods of rest so we can handle the next difficult life event thrown our way. This helps us perform well at work, check off the next item on our to-do list, and interact nicely with the next little person interrupting our day (ahem).

When our fight-or-flight response is left on too long, our bodies malfunction. We wear out and shut down—either disengaging with life (flight) or reacting aggressively to life stressors (fight). Hormones get out of balance, energies are depleted past the ability to renew quickly (or at all), and we feel disconnected and unable to handle it all. We must take proper measures and learn how to turn off our stress switch in healthy ways to be productive and thrive in the long run.

* * *

Maybe you feel like you have no time to refuel. Maybe you feel guilty taking time to refuel, so you don't! But if you don't take time to stop and refuel, eventually you will run out of gas and be forced to stop wherever the nearest gas station is. This not only requires more time and effort to get back on the road again, but it's ten times more inconvenient! Even professional NASCAR racers stop in the middle of their race to refuel, knowing they won't make it to the finish line unless they take a few precious minutes to fill up.

Maybe you do take time to refuel, but do you feel rested and rejuvenated? Are the activities you're choosing really helping you de-stress? Do you feel empowered to tackle the next hard thing?

Some activities have the appearance of being restful but provide no rejuvenating energy. Activities we tend to think are relaxing—television, scrolling through Facebook, checking out to our phones, playing video games—are said to increase our stress tanks.[1]

These activities put our minds and bodies into a state of depletion, not rejuvenation. There's a difference.

Personally, it took me a while to realize that I combat stress best through reading a creative fiction book (where I can get lost in the story), exercising, and journaling my thoughts. So I try to ensure that I am doing these things regularly to rest from that constant place of stress.

You may not figure it out right away, but I encourage you to explore certain activities and see how they affect your stress levels, because being in a constant state of stress is no way to live.

* * *

"Do not be anxious about anything, but in every situation, by prayer and petition, with thanksgiving, present your requests to God. And the peace of God, which transcends all understanding, will guard your hearts and your minds in Christ Jesus" (Phil. 4:6–7).

"Do not be anxious about **anything**..."

This sounds too good to be true, right? How can you not be anxious about anything?

Well, you learned earlier that anxiety equals fear.

When we look more deeply at every situation we are anxious or stressed about, it boils down to one of four fears.

• We fear we won't meet our deadlines = Fear of failure

While we may fear failure and experience it ourselves, in God's eyes we are never a failure. We will always find our way through Him.

> "Trust in the LORD with all your heart and lean not on your own understanding; in all your ways submit to Him, and He will make your paths straight." (Prov. 3:5–6)

• We fear connecting with another person intimately = Fear of rejection

While we may fear rejection from others, God will never reject those who love Him.

> "As you come to him, a living stone rejected by men but in the sight of God chosen and precious." (1 Peter 2:4, ESV)

- We fear sending our children off to school = Fear of loss

While we may fear loss, and even experience loss ourselves, God's eternal hope is higher than life itself.

> "So we fix our eyes not on what is seen, but on what is unseen, since what is seen is temporary, but what is unseen is eternal." (2 Cor. 4:18)

- We fear an economic crash in the future = Fear of no control

While we may fear the unknown future, God knows and His purposes for you are good.

> "'For I know the plans I have for you,' declares the Lord, 'plans to prosper you and not to harm you, plans to give you hope and a future.'" (Jer. 29:11)

While these examples may not exactly line up with yours, think through the situations you're stressed about right now and see if they connect to one of these fears. I think you will find that they do.

Let me tell you bluntly: these fears are lies from the enemy. They are not truth. How do I know? By going back to God's Word, which tells us what is true.

God's Word in Isaiah says, "Do not fear, for I am with you" (41:10). In all things, you have nothing to fear. God is by your side. Say that out loud again and again.

So, if anxiety stems from fear, and God's Word says we have nothing to fear, then there must be a way for us to not be anxious about anything, right?

You're doubting. I can almost hear your thoughts… "There's so much going on in my life. You have no idea what I'm going through!" You're right. I don't! But I don't have to.

Or perhaps it's not the weight of brokenness you're struggling under, but rather the weight of embracing your anxiety, maybe even flippantly declaring you are "stressed, blessed, and coffee obsessed!"

Without trying to sound insensitive or preachy, these are two extremes that simply come from accepting the lie that anxiety is normal, and change is hopeless. I know; I've been there too. Those lies keep you focused on the external stressors around you, which are typically outside your ability to change or control. And those stressors seem to validate the lies. But you *can* change—your internal stress mechanisms, that is—which is a good thing! You can positively change the way you think and react to stressful situations by recalling the powerful truth of God's Word to help dissipate those stress-filled moments.

However, it doesn't come naturally. It's a process that happens through prayer. The passage I referred to earlier is the ticket to understanding how we can do this better: "Do not be anxious about anything, but in every situation, by **prayer** and **petition**, with **thanksgiving**, present your **requests** to God. And the **peace** of God, which transcends all understanding, will guard your hearts and your minds in Christ Jesus" (Phil. 4:6–7).

CLASP AND CAST (PRAY AND PETITION)

"Do not be anxious about anything, but in every situation, by **prayer**…"

Are you feeling stressed out? Start praying. Pray "and **petition**," or bring all your struggles to God. Whatever is heavy on your heart, lay it all out there for Him to hear. That's what I finally did when I was at my lowest, struggling with depression. I got real, honest, and gave it to Him straight up. I told God everything I was feeling regardless of how it sounded.

EXPRESS (THANKS)

Once you get it all out, focus on the next part…"with **thanksgiving**." What can you thank God for right now? Can you pray with a heart in expectation that God will give you what you need to overcome your present situations and circumstances? It takes time and practice to think this way. So just start with something simple for now (your house, food, kids, job, school, the sunrise, a friend's text), and over time I bet your thankfulness to God will grow until you are blown away by how much you have to be thankful for.

REQUEST (PRESENT)

Next... "**present** your requests to God." Here comes the tricky part. I'm *all* about praying bold prayers to God. I think praying big prayers in faith that God will act can be a really *good* thing! In this text, however, we are asked to acknowledge in our prayers that God is in control of the outcome, He knows ahead of time what's ultimately best, and we must trust Him to act accordingly. Presenting our requests carries the idea that we are to offer these prayers to Him without ultimatum, trusting He will handle them wisely and with love. Even though we are requesting or presenting Him with what we want, we must remember He's in control. It may not make sense to you at the time, but hopefully you will start to see how God works all things out for our good to those who love Him (Romans 8:28).

Are you praying for your husband to get that job? Go for it! But know that if he doesn't get it, God has something better in mind.

Praying for God to heal you from an illness? It's totally possible! But if He doesn't, perhaps His purpose in this is to help you grow deeper in intimacy and reliance on Him through this rather than zapping you with miraculous healing (although that can happen). He wants more than anything that you don't miss the powerful opportunity to grow in your intimacy with Christ, inspiring others to Jesus through your incredible trust in Him despite your circumstances.

Praying for more patience with your kids? Don't be surprised if God brings *more* opportunities to practice patience with them.

While stressful circumstances may not subside right away, or ever, you can experience internal change in such a way your heart remains at peace amid those stressful situations. Pray wisely. Pray not only for changed surroundings but for a change of heart as you continue to believe in the powerful ability of the Holy Spirit working in and through you to rise above every situation.

CALM (PEACE AND TRUST)

"Then the **peace** of God which transcends all understanding will **guard** your hearts and your minds in Christ Jesus." This is where we discover a beautiful promise. Through this prayer of petitioning and presenting our requests, we will receive a peace that really does surpass all understanding, when just moments ago our anxious thoughts were getting the best of us. What does that mean exactly? It means you can have God's peace even in stressful circumstances. It means your current circumstances do not have to dictate your stress levels. While situations and circumstances can't always change, our hearts can. Are you still tracking with me?

I want you to notice that this is an *active* promise, which means that God is the one actively doing the work. He promises you His peace. He promises that His peace will actively guard your heart and mind. This is why you can find peace when you're facing crazy, difficult, heart-wrenching circumstances. As you submit your fears at Jesus's feet, the paralyzing fear disperses, and your heart is guarded by God's peace.

* * *

This is a lot to digest! But it is important to break down these four fears, dismantling them with God's truth by bringing you through applicable Biblical passages and my own personal stories to help you see the deeper truths that will set you free!

God loves me; He doesn't reject me.
God is for me; not against me.
God is eternal; this is temporary.
God is in control; He knows what's best for me.

When stress rises, pray! But don't pray just any prayer. Cast everything onto Him, remembering the truth of His Word as it "guards our hearts and minds in Christ Jesus." Use this to help you remember what to do when stressful or dark situations arise:

CLASP (pray)

▼

CAST (petition)

▼

EXPRESS (thanks)

▼

REQUEST (present)

▼

CALM (peace/trust)

Recently I felt like a failure because I went on a low dose of anti-anxiety and anti-depression medication. For years I've managed stress through therapy, reciting God's Word over and over again, and using practical ways to de-stress. While all of this helped immensely (at times I thought I was completely cured), a new season hit, and I found my anxiety and depression barging in again no matter what I did. I needed more help.

This time, help came to me in the form of a tiny pink pill I take every day now, enabling me in this season to keep doing the work God has called me to do instead of curling up in a fetal position on my bed in tears. It has prevented further panic attacks. It has helped me connect with my kids and husband more, which I'm forever grateful for. I'm going to be able to finish this book because my brain has enough of the chemicals it needs to think more clearly. Praise the Lord!

I believe in Jesus and I believe He can heal me from this in an instant. But I also believe in science and thank God for the gift of medicine to help me out when I really, truly need it. This may be the continual thorn in my flesh I'm meant to bear. But this thorn has helped me empathize with those struggling with anxiety and depression, compelling me to help in whatever ways I can.

Friend, you're not alone. You're not less of a Christian because you struggle with anxiety and depression. God hasn't given up on you. He will help you refine away your unhealthy thinking patterns that are causing so much of your anxiety. Don't be afraid to ask for help from Him or pursue help from others, so you can faithfully pursue your calling to be a loving wife, mom, friend, daughter, sister, or leader in your field.

Borrow This Refining Prayer When Words Are Few

Father God, I never realized how much these subtle sin areas I hold back from You are keeping me from experiencing more fully the magnitude of Your love for me. But I'm aware of them now. Help me to turn away from the things of this world that aren't healthy for my heart and soul, and help me instead pursue the things You know are best for me. Give me a heart to want to love You better instead of a heart that is complacent to my sin. I am sorry for turning my eyes, heart, and mind against You at times. I'm so thankful that though I don't deserve it, You extend unconditional grace and love to me. Help me love You more so I can love myself more and in turn love others more. This is the greatest of your commands and this is my goal for life: to love You with all my heart, mind, and soul, and love others as I love myself. You are a good, good Father—patient, caring, grace-giving. Refine the areas that are holding me back. In Jesus's name, amen.

Section 3

RESTORE

He makes me lie down in green pastures.
He leads me beside still waters. He
restores my soul. He leads me in paths of
righteousness for his name's sake.

Psalms 23:2–3, ESV

CHAPTER 9

Who Is God Really?

No words would come. The darkness clouding me was too dense. I'd experienced dark seasons in my life before, when permanent indentations formed in the carpet beside my bed where I knelt in prayer.

This season was different.

My experience with depression affected every area of my life: physically, emotionally, socially, and, yes...spiritually. Instead of presenting my happy, bubbly self, I retreated from friends and cried. All. The. Time. I couldn't snap out of it as my husband so "gently" encouraged me to do. I wanted to, but it wasn't that easy.

When my husband asked me to pray with him each night, I always declined. I just couldn't. Wouldn't. Didn't. My heart was resistant to it. No, worse than that. It had encased itself in what felt like an impenetrable, waterproof wall lowered to a depth of ten million feet. It was during this season I was thankful to have the powerful prayers of

my husband and many friends when my mouth couldn't utter a single word.

* * *

Over the next year, God brought key people into my life
whom He used through their grace and honest conversation to help me overcome my battle with depression. My
husband picked up slack around the house, gave me more
days to rest, and encouraged me to get together with my
girlfriends even though some days it was hard. But it was
good. I needed a bit of a push sometimes from him to do
what I needed to do to get my mind well again.

God used many people to help me sort through my
thoughts, exposing the false beliefs, lies, and sinful areas
in my life that were holding me back from experiencing
the love, joy, fullness, and intimacy with God I desperately
needed in order to get healthy again. The most significant
relationship He blessed me with was meeting an incredibly
wise counselor. Through her encouragement to invest in
self-reflection and spiritual growth by reading God's Word
once again, I came to realize that most of my depression
episodes and the distance I felt from God stemmed from
my inability to separate truth from lies, blinding me from
the truth. From rejection by friends, to failed business ven-
tures, to feeling lost in my marriage, to feeling hopeless
about the future, the voices in my head were anything but
truthful—their messages left a wake of depression and anxiety and pain trailing through my life:

You are such a failure.
You're never going to have any close friends.
Your marriage sucks; you should give up.
Nobody cares about you or your future.

In these seasons, I could see how saturated I was in false, negative thinking about my identity, creating in me a warped view of God. I wasn't saturated in God's truth, and because of this, I had a tough time wanting to pray or communicate to a God I felt like I couldn't trust. I had bought into the lies that God wasn't good, God didn't care, and God wouldn't extend me the same grace He extends to everyone else. These other voices were growing louder and louder, tainting the truth. So much so, in fact, I began to think these were things God was telling me:

I (God) am so disappointed in you.
I (God) will never give you any close friends.
I (God) won't be able to help you.
I (God) don't care about you or your future.

These are lies. All of them. Lies we have such an easy time believing about ourselves. Lies we end up believing if we don't guard our minds and hearts through God's truth. The truth is this:

God can turn your failure into good (Prov. 3:5–6).
God will never reject you (1 Peter 2:4).
God is trustworthy (2 Cor. 4:18).
God is in control and knows what's best for you (Jer. 29:11).

Knowing the truth of God's identity for you and His view of you will help you understand who you really are. It will unpack your unique purpose and activate your callings as you draw yourself nearer to Him. Don't let your depressed emotions override the truthful devotions shared in Scripture that tell you the truth of who God really is.

We need to remember something: there are going to be times when our emotions fight with our beliefs. We may feel conflicted because our emotions may want to tell us one thing while our faith is fighting to bring us back to the truth of who God really is. This happens a lot when we explore the character of God in the Bible and compare it to the experiences we are facing.

The Shack, a book that was turned into a movie in 2017, unpacks the character of God. It's a story of a man named Mack whose daughter is tragically killed, and he spirals into a deep depression in which he questions his innermost beliefs about God. He enters a crisis of faith, and then receives a mysterious letter urging him to go to a shack in the mountains. Mack journeys to this shack and encounters a supernatural experience where he meets the Trinity of God. Through this meeting, Mack begins to understand the depth of God's character through his interactions with Him and faces the lies he was believing about God.

At one point, he meets with Wisdom, and in the core of the mountains, they have a heated discussion about how God determines justice. She gives Mack the role of God and asks him to start making decisions as if he were God himself. Walking him through various scenarios, Wisdom finally takes Mack's two remaining children and asks him to choose which one to send to hell and which one to send to heaven for their wrongdoings. "I want you to choose which one will spend eternity in heaven, and which one in hell," Wisdom calmly but firmly says.

Pausing, Mack says, "I . . . I can't."

"Why not? I'm only asking you to do what you believe God does. So who will go to hell?"

"I can't." Mack refuses.

"You must," Wisdom insists.

"This isn't fair."

Forced to decide, Mack surrenders and says, "Take me. I'll go instead of them."

A knowing smile graces Wisdom's lips. She explains to Mack that this is exactly what God did. God sacrificed Himself by taking our place, paying the price of our sins so that we wouldn't have to. We are free from our sins because of the sacrifice God made for us through Jesus. When we trust and believe that Jesus paid this penalty for us, we are saved.

The truth is: we are God's children. God wants us to be with Him in heaven. Yes, even the prostitute, murderer, child abductor. As hard as it is to believe this of someone pursuing such dark acts in this world, they are children of God too. This beautiful reminder demonstrates the justice of God and the deep, abiding love of God. It's true for each and every one of us. However, not everyone chooses to believe in their heavenly identity, and instead they choose a worldly identity—partnering with the enemy instead.

Multiple times in my life, my mind and circumstances war with what I've declared to be true:

When my niece of seventeen died by suicide, I had a hard time believing God was still just.

When my friend of three young boys lost her husband unexpectedly, I had a hard time believing God was still good.

When my coaching client shared that her husband had an affair and they were pursuing divorce, I had a hard time believing God was still loving.

We all face a crisis of belief at some point, yet we fail to discuss it. We silently wrestle with the truths of God's character that we've been taught to believe. We wrestle with Scripture when it says:

God is just. "The Rock! His work is perfect, For all His ways are just" (Deut. 32:4, AMP).

God is good. "Oh, taste and see that the Lord is good! Blessed is the man who takes refuge in him!" (Psalm 34:8, ESV).

God is love. "Whoever does not love does not know God, because God is love" (1 John 4:8).

This is the point where you need to ask yourself, *Am I going to believe God is who He says He is despite my circumstances and emotions?*

What helps me process the truth about God's identity is walking through the Psalms and writing out God's character in the margins of my journaling Bible. For example, when I read a passage that says: "For the LORD watches over the way of the righteous" (Psalm 1:6), I can identify the truth that God watches over me. I dug deeper into the original Hebrew language of this text and discovered that the word for "watches" is *yodea*, which means to know deeply and fully. God has a deep knowing of each of His children. He knows you. He knows me. How wonderful is it to be deeply and fully known!

When I struggle with depression, I have a hard time believing I'm known, significant, or loved. I succumb to my emotions and the lies that tell me I'm not worth pursuing. The distance I feel comes when I believe the lies that He has given up on me and that the love I was lacking was because He was disappointed in me.

But God didn't give up on me. He hasn't given up on you either, and He never will! He loves you despite what your emotions say to you in this hard season. He knows you despite the loneliness you feel in your heart right now. He is for you, even though the whole world may feel against you right now. Go back to His Word, to remember what is true.

A NEW NAME

Another element that radically changed my life is something that may feel a bit odd at first.

All throughout Scripture, you read about people who encounter God powerfully, and then God changes their name. Abram became Abraham. Sarai was changed to Sarah. Saul was transformed to Paul. There's significance in new names. There's power and a deep feeling of being known by God through this new name they each experience. There's a passage that hints at this as well: "To him who overcomes, to him I will give some of the hidden manna, and I will give him a white stone, and a *new name* written on the stone which no one knows but he who receives it" (Rev. 2:17, NKJV, emphasis added).

When I went to the retreat seven months pregnant with my daughter and struggling in my depression, I was encouraged to ask God if perhaps He had another name for me. The speaker shared that God had revealed that her name was "shooting star," which confirmed so many parts about her character. For example: her spur-of-the-moment mentality and the way she lights up the room with her personality. It took months of patiently asking and listening for God to respond, but when He did, she felt all the pieces of understanding fall into place through this name.

I asked half-heartedly for a new name. I didn't really believe God would respond and felt a little silly asking. I thought it would take months (if at all) to hear from Him or get any sort of inclination that God was speaking a new name for me.

One afternoon at the retreat, I was sitting on the beautiful farmhouse porch. The entire premises were covered in roses of assorted colors—flowing around the buildings, walkways, and this large wraparound porch. Closing my eyes, I tuned my ears to the hum of the bees, the singsong of finches, and the slight rustling of the breeze cooling my skin. As I prayed, I could sense God asking me to open my eyes. When I did, bursting into view were butterflies of vivid colors fluttering from rose to rose.

Suddenly the bell rang, signaling the next session. Worship music began to play in the large barn where our meetings were held. I stepped down off the porch and walked into the barn. I found a spot and continued standing as I worshiped God. I cannot remember the name of the song, but I remember the words had to do with receiving a new name. My thoughts traveled again to my silent prayer: *God, I'm still curious, what is my name? Do you even have one for me?*

Firmly in my mind, I heard Him say, *I already showed you.* The image of a butterfly flashed through my thoughts, and I felt immediate confirmation to my question. *No way, Lord! There's no way! Perhaps I'm just wanting to be called a butterfly. I'm not really that, am I? That's not who I really am?*

But I continued to see the image of butterflies fluttering in my mind and felt the tingle of truth tugging on my heart—"God's butterfly."

For the next several years, God continued to unpack how much my character and the woman He's created me to be resemble that of a butterfly—delicate but strong, casting beautiful visions for the future, zigzagging all over the place with her passions but somehow they all line up toward a specific destination.

I hold this truth close, and inch by inch it melts the lies—you're too emotional, you're so scatterbrained, you have too many ideas and not enough execution, you're ugly. This image of a butterfly has been a reminder of who I am when my faith begins to waver. I begin to believe in my

name, which emphasizes my unique purpose and the multiple callings in life God is bringing me into.

* * *

I remember feeling doubt again about my new name a year
later as I was up against a difficult season requiring strength
I didn't feel capable of. I felt discouraged as I thought of
how dainty and weak a butterfly looks. I was giving in
to the enemy's whispers that said, *You're not strong enough
for this.* I went for a walk to our greenbelt park down the
street, mulling these thoughts in fear. The Santa Ana winds
fiercely beat against my chest and legs as I walked the path
in front of me. Buffeted by the winds but making steady
progress, I noticed movement in the corner of my eye. Fluttering crazily in the air above me was a lone butterfly—its
delicate, light wings powerfully navigating the force against
her as well. The winds took her wings here and there, but
this little jewel fought the winds and kept flying toward her
destination. It was incredible, really, watching something
seemingly so delicate and light fight the massive winds with
steady progress. I sensed God telling me, *Pay attention; this is
you too. You are stronger than you know. The storms in life will not
take you away from the destination you're meant to reach.*

There were other moments as well, tender reminders of
God's love and belief in me. I would see butterflies on win-
ter days when there shouldn't have been any. I noticed my
friend's daughter's earrings in the shape of a butterfly on an
especially difficult day. Or my daughter's shirt would, iron-

ically, have a butterfly on it when I needed this reminder most.

God continues to remind me He loves me and the truth about my character traits through something as simple and seemingly childish as a butterfly.

Maybe you need to ask God too. Ask, "What name do you have for me?" Maybe the name He gives you is Sage because of the wisdom you exude and your natural bent toward teaching. Maybe it's Hope, Quartz, or Pancake—not sure what significance Pancake would have, but who knows? The options are endless for how God might want to communicate the truth of your character to you.

But know this: I do believe God has another name specifically for you. Eventually He will reveal it to you if you're patient. This new name will help you believe in the truth of your identity in Christ.

* * *

Before I knew God personally and embraced Jesus wholeheartedly, I felt numb to any sort of direction or purpose for my life. I still remember a time in high school when I was on a beach vacation with my family. I slipped out after dark when everyone was asleep and sat on the rocky beach wall, watching the inky swells of the rolling sea. The waves boomed in the dark. I could barely make out the moon-colored churn of seafoam. The darkness felt similar to the darkness in my own life. All the pain, emptiness, loneliness, and struggles welled up in this moment with thoughts of *Maybe it would be better if I just swam as far as I could and then peacefully sank to the bottom?* I still shudder as I remember how lost and empty I felt—void of purpose. But the fear of the icy-cold, pitch-black water (I'm still a bit scared of the dark) made me think better of this idea.

I know someone reading this right now has been there. Maybe you're already there. Maybe you've been wondering this same thing and you've had those crazy thoughts swell in your head too. Maybe you've never experienced Jesus yet, or maybe you have, and you still get overwhelmed with thoughts of feeling helpless, purposeless, and alone.

You need to know you're not alone. You need to know you're not crazy to have those thoughts and still be in a relationship with Jesus at the same time. You need to know there's an enemy at war over your heart and mind right now who wants nothing more than to make you feel helpless, purposeless, and alone. We forget that we are in a spiritual battle and the emotions we feel aren't always based on truth. The One who created this world is above the thief of this world who seeks to steal, kill, and destroy us. This all-powerful God who saved the best of His creation for last is fiercely fighting for your love and protection. Your worth is greater than the rarest ruby. In fact, you are worth dying for because that's exactly what He did.

But here's the issue: many believe Jesus came for us so that we might have this greater joy in heaven. Which is partly true. But what about experiencing greater joy in life right now?

There's so much we can experience with God right now. He came so that we might have a peace that surpasses understanding when those stressful moments arise. He came so that our hearts may know our unique purpose to actively fulfill the callings He has called us to with Him. He came so that we might laugh without fear of the future. We may have to fight for it. Claim it. Stake it in the ground over our life. Restore the truth of God's identity into our hearts and minds so we know the truth about who we are in His image. We live in a world that is broken from the original design God had for it. It's not the Garden of Eden anymore. Joy, peace, and contentment aren't in totality here as they will be in heaven. But the awe-inspiring wonders of God's love and joy for us aren't invisible. They are here for the taking. Surrender to His love, believe His purpose for you, and remember what is really true: you are loved and you are never alone.

Borrow This Restoring Prayer When Words Are Few

LORD Almighty, Your Word says that You are good, just, and trustworthy. Help me believe these to be true when my emotions and circumstances fight to say otherwise. Restore my faith to the truth of Your identity and help me believe in those truths. Also, do You have a name for me? I want to believe this as Rachel believes. Please show me or speak to me this other name You have for me that reflects the person You've created me to be. In Jesus's name, amen.

CHAPTER 10

God's Not Just a Get-Out-of-Hell-Free Card

I'm driving and suddenly notice my mouth feels like cotton. I see an inviting half-empty water bottle sitting in the cup holder next to me. Grabbing it, I take a deep swig to alleviate the starchy feeling in my mouth—only to gag, nearly spitting it out all over the car! Choking it down so as not to make a mess, I now recognize this water has been sitting here far too long, giving it a metallic and lukewarm taste.

Have you ever experienced the bitter taste of stagnant, lukewarm water? It defeats the purpose of desired refreshment, doesn't it?

Stagnancy runs rampant in our culture. No, usually not when it comes to being productive in our careers, building our homes, or tending to our family. But stagnancy is in our spiritual disciplines, disciplines that can revive our hearts and release our purpose.

There was a church long ago named Laodicea whose

attendees were also lacking—neither hot nor cold in their faith (Revelation 3). They had become lukewarm at best— a self-sufficient church body of people, wealthy in material possessions, blending in with the rest of the worldly crowd, being overly prideful of their ability to need absolutely nothing. They looked successful on the outside, boasting through selfies on Instagram and Facebook with their wealthy church programs, priding themselves on being "hip" with the rest of the crowd. They assimilated to the cultural norms so as not to ruffle any feathers, looking neither zealous nor completely dead. Okay, perhaps the part about the selfies was *my own* modern-day exaggerated view of this church, but suffice it to say I think it's a close parallel.

I bet there are many of us who can relate to this complacency of our own faith that these church members thousands of years ago had as well. Can you? I know I can.

Perhaps you attend church on Sundays merely to check off your "spiritual checklist" because that's what a good Christian does. Or you go to work and blend in with the rest of the crowd so as not to look overly spiritual. After church group, you attend happy hour, getting a few too many drinks with your non–faith-filled friends while sharing F-bombs in your banter with them—it's a wonder they even see you as a believer. Or maybe you think about how great it is when others go out and serve the community through service projects, yet that's just not your cup of tea. You become indifferent, too busy creating a self-made life of comforts and pursuing your own agenda, often to the detriment of your soul.

We allow our own self-sufficiency to take over instead of allowing a God-sufficient perspective to penetrate our lives. We create a false reality that we don't really need God in our lives, except as a get-out-of-hell-free card. Sometimes other things take our focus away from what we need most. We allow desire for wealth, fame, or success to creep onto our priority lists, leaving us "too busy" to grow in our faith. You stop desiring to read God's Word, stop praying, and stop serving others in your church because "life is too busy" for God to take priority. You still believe in God, will still go to heaven, so why does it matter?

Because God despises the lukewarm: "So, because you are lukewarm—neither hot nor cold—I am about to spit you out of my mouth" (Rev. 3:16).

The people of this Laodicean church assimilated with the culture around them—they integrated, adapted, conformed—instead of permeating the culture with their love and belief in Jesus. They became complacent in their spiritual walk with Christ, allowing other things of the world or their own selfish desires to take priority over Christ. They became lukewarm, which was abhorrent to God.

* * *

When we spend more time thinking about ourselves and pursuing our own desires, our spiritual muscles become stagnant. When we avoid spending time with God, digging into His Word, forgetting to communicate with Him through prayer regularly, letting go of the active part of our faith, and lacking the desire to come together as the body of Christ, we become spiritually weak (1 Cor. 12:27). We need each other as believers to sharpen one another as iron sharpens iron. We need to be encouraged by one another as God designed community with Him to be.

But when we stop doing our part for His kingdom work here on earth (whether big or small), in turn our faith grows stagnant and lukewarm. We become content with sitting on the sidelines drinking our stale water, allowing others to do the work God invited us to do, forgoing the soul-filling experiences God desires us to have!

Friend, God is not just a get-out-of-hell-free card. There's so much more to this life when we pursue Jesus with our whole heart, following His ways and pursuing purposeful work with Him. When we read His Word, it becomes alive in us as we fulfill the impossible with God, made possible with Him. When we obey the Holy Spirit's invitations, we experience a deeper, more fulfilling life than the premade life the world offers us. When we communicate with God—just start talking to Him when you are driving through the carpool line, walking through the grocery store, driving home from work, taking a walk with your dog—we will start to see and experience God differently in our everyday life. He is real. His presence is alive in us. He communicates to our hearts if we still our minds enough to hear His voice: "Be still, and know that I am God" (Psalm 46:10, NLT). "The Lord will fight for you, and you have only to be silent" (Exodus 14:14, ESV).

Can we agree that lukewarm water is disgusting to drink? Stagnant water sitting in a marsh flares our nostrils with its stench. Drink it, and it will make you sick.

God calls us to be a group of people who actively display love, joy, peace, patience, kindness, goodness, faithfulness, gentleness, and self-control (Galatians 5:22–23). He calls us believers to be in the world—permeating Christ's love to others—but not of the world—conforming to the world's standards for living a life fully dependent on ourselves and according to our selfish motives (Romans 12:2). The more God's Word pours into you, the more His refreshing spirit will flow out of you. Do not assimilate. Do not segregate. Radiate. Be an example of the richness of God's love and salvation in your life.

It's time for you to get off the sidelines with your self-sufficiency and complacent faith.

DON'T PUT GOD IN A BOX

I hear this all the time: "I don't have time to pray or read my Bible."

I get it. We live in the fastest paced society at this moment in time right now. I feel it. My inbox is always screaming for the attention from others. I see it. Our schedules are packed to the brim with kids' soccer tournaments, grocery shopping, birthday parties, meetings, work.

But what if you knew what you're missing with Him when you make Him your last priority? What if you knew how powerful God's Word and presence is when you seek those spiritual moments with Him?

What if I told you that you needed to wake up on Monday at 4:45 a.m. because otherwise you will be permanently bedridden for the rest of your life by 5:00 a.m. if you don't. You would get up no matter what, wouldn't you? Or what if I told you to be at the courthouse by 9:30 a.m.; otherwise your children will be taken away from you forever. You'd do everything in your power to be there, arriving early just to make sure you got through traffic, right? I know this sounds drastic and far-fetched, but it packs a relevant point. When we forgo making time to feed our hearts and minds—reading His Word, praying, and practicing stillness to hear and act on the Holy Spirit's invitations—we are killing our soul by starving it of necessary spiritual food, energy, and nourishment.

I know this to be true. Not long ago, I had to ask myself again, *Why am I feeling distant from you, God?*

Assessing myself honestly, I could see how busy I'd become with the move we'd made in September 2018 from California to Idaho. I failed to make the time and effort to dig into my Bible more than twice in the previous month because of the stress of that season. My prayer life wasn't consistent. I hadn't sat in stillness long enough to hear what God wanted to speak to me about. I lacked in journaling with God where I tended to sense God's presence and write out reminders of His love for me. I failed to show up to "coffee dates" with Him, so to speak, and because of this, my relationship with Him was lacking. And while I understand and admit why I felt distant from Him, I needed to remember I could always start again.

I used to think God needed my perfect devotion to Him, otherwise it would all be useless. I'd make New Year's resolutions to read the Bible in one year, but then give up on day forty-six because I was behind and didn't do it perfectly.

It's not about perfection. It's about active progression toward Him.

I put God in a box when it came to my meetings with Him—my "quiet times." I'd set aside a five-minute window to read His word and pray, then forget about Him the rest of the day. I didn't think I could have an intimate experience with Jesus without a designated time of quiet, without music and candles that made the Holy Book sparkle in front of me (Hollywood Christianity, right?). While taking time in stillness for God is important and healthy, what if we practiced connecting with God like He's with us all the time?

This is what I do now. In the mornings while my kids are scarfing down their breakfast, I open my devotional book out on the crumb-covered counter and snag a few lines of His truth. Sure, an interruption is inevitable ("Mom, can I have more milk? Can you get me a napkin?"), but I expect this, so it doesn't frustrate me. And when a seemingly non-busy moment presents itself again (everyone chewing), I read a few more lines. It doesn't feel like much, but it's been amazing to notice how much the state of my soul is changed by even a few moments of intentional connection.

I don't stop there, though. I pray in the car on my way to drop my kids off at school, talking to God about what's on my heart. I listen to worship music on the way home. I even pray in the shower. Sometimes I just dwell on one passage of Scripture for the entire day, mulling it over and over again. I chew on the deeper meaning of "taste and see that the Lord is good; blessed is the one who takes refuge in him" (Psalm 34:8). Even amid great tragedy and sadness in this world (or the frustrations of a driver cutting me off), I look for hints of goodness in the day—a text from a friend checking in, a gorgeous sunrise, hot chai lattes, clean clothes (but never put away). When I feel stressed or overwhelmed, I say a quick prayer of peace and notice (often within minutes) how God meets me in that prayer as I take refuge in Him.

Surprisingly, even though I'm not spending gobs of time with Him in quiet, my intimacy with Jesus has expanded. I feel nearer to Him. I'm drawn to Him. I find myself constantly talking to Him—mini-prayers and conversations going out to Him all throughout the day.

I didn't think these interrupted moments of devotional or Scripture reading were working until I began noticing the state of my revived heart. I didn't think God would respond to me in those scattered mini-prayer thoughts—so ineloquent—but now I sense and hear God speaking to me more and more. I've become more familiar with His voice the more time I've spent knowing Him.

I've concluded something powerful and perspective altering: "Christian quiet time" is less about time given and more about thoughtful intention.

Sure, designated times of stillness through prayer with longer periods of soaking in God's Word are powerful and effective. This is a practice I keep and use regularly as well. But to believe that this is the *only* way to have a "quiet time" and grow in our relationship with God limits God and the depth of relationship we can have with Him in less drawn-out ways.

I see this parallel in my relationship with my husband. While longer periods of time with him are wonderful and develop our love relationship (and are still necessary), our relationship is more often built upon those seemingly insignificant moments of brief interactions—a hug, a short text saying "I love you," a fifteen-minute discussion in the evening, and a positive mind-set about each other when we aren't together. These are the things that cultivate our relationship and positively connect us amidst the busyness of work, children, and other activities that fill up our time.

God wants a relationship, not your religion. He wants you to want Him instead of feeling forced. But sometimes wanting Him comes out of *duty* for Him. Sometimes we need to practice the presence of God through reading His Word, praying, and devoting times of stillness with Him to get us to a place where we see the need for Him once again.

There was a distinct switch in my heart and mind a few years ago that led me to this new understanding and desire to *want* to do these spiritual disciplines of reading, praying, and seeking Him instead of feeling required to do it. I was no longer doing it out of duty or what I would get out of it (like getting gold stars from Jesus), but after practicing these spiritual disciplines more and more, my mind-set shifted from duty to desired devotion, making this time spent with Him that much richer and more enjoyable.

Until you make that switch in your mind, where your joy comes from an overflow of love for Christ in which you say: "I *want* to pray and read my Bible and connect with God in a personal way, because I love Him and want to get to know more of His love," you will continually pick up and lay down the task of praying and reading over and over again. And yet this is the refine-and-restore process I'm facing once again: stripping away the lie that spending time with God is a boring duty instead of a joy-filled time of devotion.

I've also had to be careful about making it only about what I get out of the relationship. It needs to be about a desire to love God and grow in your relationship with Him, by praying and reading the Bible. When I don't refine my thinking to this truth, I continue to fall short, and it continues to feel like a chore. I guarantee if you had a coffee date with Oprah, Ellen, or a famous person you love, you would be jumping up and down for your chance to spend time with this person. This is how we should react to our time spent with God. "Hey, I'm literally meeting with the Creator of the universe today! Wow!" It takes an active mental commitment to restore the truth: you need Him, *and* you want Him.

You want God to be first in your life. You say He is first. But in the quiet places of your heart, ask yourself the honest question: do you truly love Him for Him? Is God the first priority in your life because you love Him and desire to be with Him? If so, it wouldn't be so hard to invest time into growing in that love relationship with Him: praying, reading the Bible, listening, and responding to His Spirit in your life.

Like a dating relationship with someone you really like, which then turns into love, it's hard *not* to want to spend every waking minute with that person. Your desire to spend time with them overrides other obligations, people, and things—sometimes to a fault. But guess what? It's never a fault to spend more time with God.

I don't always do this perfectly, but I must come to a place where I realize this Christian faith walk is not about me. It's not about simply pressing a button and receiving an entry ticket to heaven. There is more to life besides getting this heavenly token. It's about a relationship with God, Jesus, the Holy Spirit—a triune relationship (John 1:14)—experiencing His presence here on this gravity-filled earth now. Our life is not about checking off a to-do list you think you need to do for God in order to be accepted, loved, and adored. God doesn't go by the list of "ten things you need to do to be a good Christian and be accepted by God." God doesn't *need* us to pray or read our Bible for Him. He is already madly and deeply in love with us, just for us, and is complete without us (Acts 17:24–35). He simply knows that when we connect with Him using the spiritual disciplines He's created for us, it helps us to experience more of

Him and His power in our life. This restored truth about God's identity increases our spiritual vitality toward Him. And that's when our spirit comes alive.

He created us and kept us because He wanted us, and He still wants us with all of our flaws and failures. He does not need us. That is true love, my friends. God simply desires us to love Him in return, out of a desire to love Him—a reciprocal relationship of true love.

> *Whoever does not love does not know God, because God is love. This is how God showed his love among us: He sent his one and only Son into the world that we might live through him.* (1 John 4:8–9)

When you let these truths sink in, everything starts to change. You see God differently. You see glimpses of the adventure God is beckoning you to pursue with Him. You will hear His Voice more powerfully and more consistently in your life when you keep pursuing Him first. And ultimately, this will propel you to do things with God you never thought possible.

Borrow This Restoring Prayer When Words Are Few

Heavenly Father, I'm starting to see the truth of Your character and actually believe it too. Help me to believe You are good when life doesn't feel good to me. Help me to believe You are just when the injustices of the world creep in. Help me to believe You are loving when I don't feel loved. Help me to believe You have a beautiful path and plan for me when the road of my life takes a detour I didn't want. I will keep reciting Scripture over in my mind, so the shouts of the enemy become less noticeable. I know this takes work, every day, to remember and believe in Your truths. I may falter, but I will continue to fight for the truth to penetrate my mind over the lies. I'm thankful someday we will get to meet face-to-face, but until then there is so much abundant life to live for in the here and now. Thank you, Lord, for these truths. In Jesus's name, amen.

Section 4

RELEASE

Now faith is the assurance of things
hoped for, the convictions of things not
seen.

Hebrews 11:1, ESV

CHAPTER 11

A Vibrant Life

My words penetrated the air with truth: "I just feel so disconnected from you." My shrugging shoulders hinted at it, and my hefty sigh confirmed it.

My husband, Jeff, reached his hands over my plate of sushi rolls to my fingers. I looked at him, picking at my cuticles. He looked at me with eyes that said, *I'm going to fix this.*

For the next seven days he made a valiant effort: sending me notes, responding to my text messages, and listening to me chat about my day. At our next dinner date out, he felt confident he'd get a different response from me. But he was met again with "I just feel so disconnected from you still."

At this point you're probably wondering, *Girl, what's wrong with you? He is trying so hard and sounds like a prince!*

But a key piece was missing. While I was pouring out my heart to my husband, he failed to open his heart to me. While he did a lot of things for me that were sweet, lovely, and showed he cared, there was a wall around his heart, keeping us from a deeper intimacy that I needed to experience with him. He would give me just enough of him, but not reveal the deeper parts of him that I desired most. When I asked him questions, I would get short responses. He failed to share the vulnerable parts of his soul with me. I wanted his whole heart, not just the outer layers of it. I was continually giving him my all but felt a vacancy and barrier in his. There's more to a relationship than just doing things for each other. You must let each other in. That's true love and intimacy, my friend.

We do this a lot. We tend to learn a lot about God and do a lot of things for God, but we fail to let Him into the deeper recesses of our own heart. God is actively pouring out His love on us, has opened Himself up to us, sacrificed His life for us, and yet we love Him just enough to feel good about ourselves and reap a few benefits but not enough to give our whole hearts to Him. We're afraid to show Him *all* of us, and settle instead for just the Instagram reel version. This leaves us feeling distant from Him when, really, we are distancing ourselves from Him—even if we don't mean to.

For a relationship to thrive and grow, both have to open their hearts and expect deeper intimacy. It takes two willing hearts.

* * *

I joke when I say that my Jacuzzi saved my marriage, but it's kind of true.

The day after I found out I was pregnant with twins,

I went into major nesting mode. Although my husband wasn't ready to buy a home, my three-year hobby search for homes in prime areas of Southern California finally went into high drive. An attractive short sale popped up on the market in my dream area to live in, at a great price. Even though it was still a bit pricier than what Jeff wanted to spend, he was open to "just look at it." So of course, we went that weekend to "just look," and much to my delight we ended up signing papers the next day!

The house had a gorgeous pool with a fantastic Jacuzzi attached. This was one thing my husband did not want in a home. I get it. The maintenance and costs associated with a pool alone will break the bank. But the benefits it brought to our life and marriage was like paying for weekly marriage counseling each month!

When our twins arrived, date nights became few and far between. Without family nearby to help, we had to get creative about how to have any sort of intimacy in our demanding and exhausting life.

Many evenings, we would bring our baby monitor to the blue-tiled spa edge at the golden hour of eight o'clock when our twins were blissfully asleep. It was at this time we could sink into the steaming bubbles for a good hour without interruption. This soaking time brought out the best of both worlds for us: it prompted deeper conversation (much to my delight) and usually ended in some steamy marriage interaction (much to his delight).

I can't help but think how similar this is to what our relationship with God is supposed to look like. Okay, just to be clear, I'm *not* talking about the steamy interaction part. But the connection of both of our hearts—sharing the struggles, triumphs, fears, dreams for the future—that cultivates a deeper, more intimate relationship with each other.

We need to be willing to show God the subtle, weaker areas of our hearts that we often hide from Him, and enter with more repentance so we can experience more of His grace-filled redemption. Do you give Him only the shiny parts of your life but hide away the unsightly parts, stuffing them in a closet somewhere? Maybe you think, *Well, He already knows and sees this. Why do I have to verbally or mentally share this with Him if He already knows?* Yes, God knows everything about you. He doesn't need you to share your regrets. He knows. He doesn't need you to share your dreams. He created you to dream. But He knows that when we share everything with Him—our sorrows, our joys, our failures, our questions—it brings *repentance* to our souls, it *revitalizes* our minds, and it *releases* our bodies back to His service. Ultimately, it *restores* our desire for Him and invokes deep thankfulness for His indescribable love.

Although building our relationship with God is not as tangible as sitting across from your husband in a Jacuzzi, or across from a friend over coffee, we can sense Him and feel Him through the Holy Spirit at work in our life, reading and reciting Scripture, and praying or worshiping Him, which positions us to remember His love.

THE HOLY SPIRIT IS REAL

"Is that really you, God?"

I asked myself this question when seemingly coincidental occurrences happened in my life: when I received the idea for my first book confirmed through a clear passage of Scripture. When I texted a friend who was on my heart to pray for, only to find out she had just received some painful news. When something presented itself at just the right time, I couldn't help but see the timeliness of it all.

It excites me when I experience these moments of His Spirit at work in my life—uncoincidental moments of God's undeniable presence.

However, I'm often asked, "Rachel, how do you know God is speaking to you?"

Say you're in a large, crowded area; perhaps a parade is going on. So many people and so many voices are speaking around you at the same time. Your ears perk up—you hear a familiar voice in the crowd. As you listen more closely, it sounds very much like your mom's voice! The same melodious tone with a hint of sarcasm, cascading through the other voices. Searching for the voice, you receive the confirmation you need as the crowd parts and, sure enough, there's your mom within the crowd.

What made you recognize her voice? Well, you've probably spent a lot of time with your mom. You chat with her on the phone often. Or pick any other person you've been around for a long time. Can't you pick up on the sound of their voice because of how much time you've spent knowing them? Simply being repeatedly around them and engaging in conversation with them attunes your mind to their familiar voice.

The more we spend time knowing God, pursuing God, and seeking God, the more we will recognize His voice above the other voices in the crowd.

Sometimes it can still be hard to discern. Truthfully, it takes practice to recognize His voice. In all honesty, we can't even predict how He will communicate to us. For Moses, it was a burning bush. For Esther, it was a quiet prompting. For Joseph, it was through visions. For me, it's been a combination of many different things.

God continues to affirm that I don't have to have Him (or anything in this life, for that matter) all figured out. It's impossible. We will never have Him all figured out; otherwise God would be rather boring. And predictable. And this would imply we have the mind of God, which is just silly. We are not gods and never will be; therefore we will never have His level of understanding in this life. I have no idea how He can hear and respond to billions of people every minute of every day without having a major migraine. I don't understand how He is able to keep the Earth rotating at the perfect angle at the perfect speed with the perfect distance from the sun, so we don't all burn up or freeze out. We don't understand *fully* how the Holy Spirit works because it's another dimension of God that's extremely difficult for our finite minds to process. We can understand only as much as what we read through Scripture and what's confirmed through the Holy Spirit at work in our lives.

External experiences of supernatural occurrences aren't always a guarantee of God's movement and interaction (the enemy is also at work in our lives and can be very deceiving). But to dismiss the Holy Spirit as invalid or having no real interaction in your life leaves out a fundamental way to experience deeper intimacy and awe of Him. Don't just accept what others have to say about the Holy Spirit as truth. Read the Word for yourself. The truth is there. Take off the filters and let God's Word filter directly into you first.

GOD IS SUPERNATURAL

Earlier, I shared with you my conversion story. I had a distinct encounter with the Spirit of God. I wasn't a believer until that powerful moment, which gave me the tangible evidence I needed to know God is real, the Bible is true, and He communicates with us in supernatural ways.

And yet why is this so hard to believe? If God is supernatural, can't we expect Him to do supernatural things in our lives?

What I experienced goes against anything I can explain with logic or reason. But I also can't deny what happened that night. It contradicted science but propelled me to a belief that I hadn't had just a moment before. It was a much-needed answer to my prayers and a confirmation of God's presence that I still hold close, a memory that I can turn to whenever I feel my faith wavering or I'm being attacked by others for my faith.

Personal testimony is powerful, if it aligns with what is true in Scripture. So if you have had spiritual experiences, I urge you to double-check those experiences with the Word of God and what it says, in order to know if they are from God or not.

There are multiple people in the Bible with some remarkable stories of the Spirit working in their lives. Just open the book and read story after story. Supernatural encounters with God are in almost every chapter. The Spirit of God is active and alive in and through His people, performing incredible acts that are still being performed today.

Unfortunately, there are some who say the Spirit of God is at work in their life, in order to justify making really bad, selfish decisions. For example, I had a friend claim that God wanted them to cheat on their spouse. This is contrary to what He teaches in Scripture: "You shall not commit adultery" (Ex. 20:14, ESV). The truth is that the desire to be unfaithful is never from God. The enemy of God is the one whispering the lie that adultery is okay. I've also heard others claim that stealing money or being deceitful with money to bring about financial success is okay because they are making more to donate to ministries to expand God's Kingdom. Again, this is contrary to what He teaches in Scripture: "Do not steal. Do not deceive or cheat one another" (Lev. 19:11, NLT). God is clear that this behavior, even if the money is being put back into good things—building churches, helping nonprofits, aiding the poor—is against His instructions for us and does more harm than good to our character.

There are times in my life when I thought the Holy Spirit was speaking to me or agreeing with me about something I wanted to pursue, but looking back I now see how spiritually immature I was. I can see now that those desires didn't align with God's Word. They were tainted by my own desire to go in the direction I wanted. I convinced myself that God was involved and pleased with my plans because I had a very specific plan and path that I wanted to follow.

This happened most often in my early walk with God. One such path was a business venture and becoming wealthy. In my spiritual naïveté, I thought God wanted me to pursue this, so that I could be a steward of His Kingdom in monetary ways. While being a steward financially for God's Kingdom is not wrong (we need humble believers who are generously giving to God's work), I was blinded by my own greed for money and wanted God to bless this path and plan for me. It became clear that it wasn't where the Holy Spirit was leading, much to my dismay. I can see how I fooled myself into believing that the Holy Spirit was behind it. I was so desirous of success at an early age that I convinced myself God wanted me to be successful so I could help more people financially. Thankfully, He allowed my business to fail and produced greater humility in me. "But I [Jesus] tell you I am going to do what is best for you. This is why I am going away. The Holy Spirit cannot come to help you until I leave. But after I am gone, I will send the Spirit to you" (John 16:7, CEV). In His mercy, He broke me, so I could be bound to His truth once again— "God opposes the proud but gives grace to the humble" (James 4:6, ESV)—and He rebuilt my character to become a closer reflection of Him. "Those who live according to the flesh have their minds set on what the flesh desires; but those who live in accordance with the Spirit have their minds set on what the Spirit desires. The mind governed by the flesh is death, but the mind governed by the Spirit is life and peace" (Romans 8:5–6).

What might God be withholding from you in order to refine your character and restore your identity as His image bearer? Is it possible that your own selfish desires are taking the lead over the Holy Spirit's desires for you?

God's Word is powerful; it doesn't lie. Take what you sense the Holy Spirit is telling you ("In the same way, the Spirit helps us in our weakness. We do not know what we ought to pray for, but the Spirit himself intercedes for us through wordless groans" Romans 8:26) and confirm it with God's Word, just as John says: "Dear friends, do not believe every spirit, but test the spirits to see whether they are from God, because many false prophets have gone out into the world" (1 John 4:1).

THE WORD OF GOD

It jumped off the page at me. My heart lurched, saying, *Pay attention to this!*

It was totally out of context from what the story was about. Yet the words leaped off the page at me, searing my heart with truth. They spoke instantly into what I was currently wrestling with.

Reading this timely passage of Scripture, "remember the devotion of your youth" (Jeremiah 2:2), combined with the Spirit's leading in my heart, confirmed what I was hearing: *this is the book I want you to create.* And if it hadn't been for this confirmation I needed from God's Word that what I was heading toward was in fact the Spirit leading, I never would have been propelled to write my first book—*Big and Little Coloring Devotional*—which became a national bestseller, read by thousands of families worldwide.

Has this happened to you? You read something in Scripture and it answers a question you are wrestling with? Or maybe you've asked for clarity and direction and then...boom! You come across a passage that says exactly what you need to hear.

This is how the Bible works. It's alive and active. It transforms and renews. It compels and directs. And it confirms what we think the Holy Spirit is telling us.

* * *

I used to think the Bible was rather boring. Okay, I still think there are some boring parts of the Bible (the book of Numbers, anyone?), but the more I read it, the more I see resemblances to the old stories in my own modern-day life.

Take the story of Sarah, a barren women who was past

her prime to have babies. She didn't believe God when He told her that she would have a son. In fact, she and her husband laughed at God's impossible plan for her, dismissing His ability to make this miracle a reality (Genesis 18).

Well, after a few years, nothing happened. After several years and no baby to show for it, she all but gave up on God's promise for her. In fact, she gave her husband, Abraham, over to her servant girl to make this dream move forward. Move forward it did. Her servant delivered a baby boy, but this made Sarah only more jealous since the baby wasn't hers. Sounds like Sarah had given up trusting God's promise for her. It was taking too long, Sarah believed. But thirteen years later, God's promise came true, when she gave birth to a healthy, beautiful baby boy named Isaac.

So often, I don't believe God's promises to be true. I think, *Okay, God, this is taking too long. It's time I take things into my own hands now*, which often leads to a messier and more painful experience.

Maybe you too are waiting on the promise of a baby you believe God said would come. Maybe you sense God said to take a new job in a new state, but after six months you're fired and you wonder what just happened. Maybe you sense the Spirit telling you "take that leap," only to feel the painful experience of a crash-and-burn result.

But maybe waiting for a baby was necessary to draw your heart toward a child God has for you in the foster system instead. Maybe God is refining your heart through this job loss, stripping you of pride, so that you develop a deeper layer of trust in God through this uncertainty. Maybe you didn't actually crash and burn, but you just don't see the bigger picture yet like He does.

As long as you still have breath, God is still working all things for your good. Don't stop praying even when life is strange or disappointing or hard or scary. Prayer works in so many ways to bring about your joy and God's glory. Abide in Him. He is good all the time and will never leave you. Trust Him.

THE POWER OF PRAYER

I remember being a rebellious teenager who was forced to kneel and pray every Sunday evening. I didn't see the value of it. God never seemed to answer my prayers. I always dreaded being asked to pray at the dinner table, especially because I was expected to recite prayers a specific way while including things that mustn't be left out.

Looking back, I see the heart behind my parents' forced discipline. They desired to cultivate my heart toward God through the practice of prayer in my life. However, that forced prayer practice produced a rancid taste in my mouth that lasted for the next decade. Anytime my husband would ask me to pray, I would tense up, remembering the distaste I had for praying aloud in my youth.

Over the years, God has taught me a few things about prayer. He's softened my heart and produced a real desire and excitement to pray to Him again. The way I see it, prayer is simply a conversation between you and God. He doesn't care how many "art thous" or "Father Gods" you use in your prayers. He doesn't care if you start in a certain way or recite it with style to make your prayers acceptable. He just wants you to talk to Him, acknowledge Him, and bring your requests to Him so He can work in powerful ways in your life.

When I think of prayer as having a conversation with God as if I'm talking to my best friend, all pressure comes off. Yes, a certain reverence should be recognized as we talk to the King of Creation. But I feel able to talk more openly about what I'm struggling with. I see Him as near and accessible, rather than an untouchable God of the universe. My prayer life has been more active because of this new perspective: praying in the car, when I'm prepping lunch, running errands, playing with my kids, taking a walk, or even when I file my nails. Conversational prayer with Him has increased my prayer life twenty-fold!

I see God in the everyday things of life. I notice His small and big gifts to me: a favorite worship song on the radio, a sweet hug from my daughter, my favorite paint color on the wall of my home, clean laundry, an epic sunrise, an answered prayer, a refining moment as I pray for patience, a restored moment as I learn to trust in Him again. This constant communication with God has produced a notable change in me and in the relationship I sense with Him. "Therefore confess your sins to each other and pray for each other so that you may be healed. The prayer of a righteous person is powerful and effective" (James 5:16).

So here are the three practical spiritual disciplines that have helped me revive my heart and release my purpose to Him:

1. **Pray.** It doesn't have to be eloquent. It doesn't have to be extremely intelligent. It should simply be an outpouring of your heart, an honest conversation, a desired intention to connect with Him. An easy way for me to experience Him more deeply in my prayer life has been by following this simple pattern: Revive, Refine, Restore, Release. I pray for God to *revive* my heart to want to share what's going on in my life. I pray the He will *refine* my character and strip away the things that are holding me back from enjoying deeper intimacy with Him. I pray for Him to *restore* confidence in my character and identity through understanding His character and identity. I pray to *release* my unique purpose and accept the calling by God, following Him wherever He leads.

2. **Read the Bible.** The way you continue to grow in your faith is to continue reading His Word, and apply what it says in your life. You don't have to know and understand everything; you just need to know enough for right now. Trust that God will give you understanding as you continue to read His Word for confirmation, clarity, and direction in your life.

3. **Accept the Holy Spirit's invitation.** For believers, the Holy Spirit becomes a key guide in our lives, inviting us to the path and plan God has for us. These invitations are made clearer as we pray and read His Word.

Practicing all three of these spiritual practices on a moment-by-moment basis will attune you to His presence and generate a thrill in your spirit to release your purpose as you see the miraculous workings of God in your everyday life.

Borrow This Releasing Prayer When Words Are Few

Father God, I see how important it is to practice these spiritual disciplines—prayer, reading the Bible, and accepting Your Holy Spirit's invitations to walk out the path You are beckoning me to follow. I don't want to brush off things that seem coincidental anymore. Help me recognize when You are working in my life and follow up with praise for the ways You are demonstrating your love to me. Help me be more attuned to Your voice and respond bravely. In Jesus's name, amen.

CHAPTER 12

The Truth about "Calling" and "Purpose"

I've always felt guilty for not being the mom who bakes decadent brownies and is a culinary guru in the kitchen. It's just never been my thing. It's not my gift. I'm not super passionate about cooking, although I do cook well enough to feed my tribe.

I'm not crafty either. In fact, I dreaded when the MOPS group (Moms of Pre-Schoolers) announced we were going to make Mod Podge keys that day. I got the paper stuff cut, then felt overwhelmed and unmotivated by it all, excusing myself to the bathroom instead. It's not that I hate doing crafts, but for some reason it creates anxiety in me and tends to add clutter to my home (which also stresses me out).

I used to wonder what gifts I had to offer the world, especially as a mom who didn't fit the societal norm. I read business books while my friends watch *The Bachelor*. I go outside with my wild kids in thirty-two-degree weather to find an adventure while my friends' kids quietly play happily inside. I enjoy working from home while other moms attend PTA meetings and volunteer in their kid's class.

It was only a few years ago when I began to really dig into exploring my gifts that I finally saw the value I had to offer. Discoveries that took a little over thirty years for me to make through research and books (including the Bible) helped me to figure out two main questions most women are asking today: What's my purpose? What's my calling?

PURPOSE

Let me first talk to you about purpose.

Pretend you are a cheese grater. Stay with me, I promise this is important.

Okay, so you're a cheese grater. But what if you have no idea you're a cheese grater?

You've been going through life thinking you're an apple peeler. You're constantly frustrated because you've been trying to peel apples, only to make them look like they went through a meat grinder.

You've also tried to cut and peel potatoes, but they only look like paper shredder bits.

You feel like you've tried your hand at everything: cutting strawberries, onions, and even chicken, but it all turns to mush when you try. You give up. You decide that you're just not cut out for anything. Not only that, but it's exhausting and makes you feel completely off balance to try your hand at new things, only to feel less and less fulfilled, leaving you wondering what on earth you were created for.

You think, *Why does everyone else seems to know what they're created to be and do?* You sit back feeling lifeless, useless, and unfulfilled. You listen to the lie that you don't have a special purpose in this world, and you fall into the trap: hiding in the shadow of mundane life.

* * *

Then one day, someone notices you struggling to peel another apple and they say, "Hey, I'm pretty sure you would be good at grating cheese. Have you ever tried that before?"

Pondering the assessment but still unsure, you kindly say, "That's so sweet. But I don't know; I've never really been good at anything."

She walks off, but it sparks curiosity in you as you wonder, *Maybe it's true. Maybe God is trying to tell me something.*

You remember how as a child you enjoyed grating carrots. It was a little different from cheese, but it was one thing you felt decent at and you enjoyed too. You also remember grating cheese at one point when you were young, but then one day you were given a pretty hard piece of cheese and struggled with it, so you decided to shelve that one too.

Now, deciding to test this out, you go to a banquet and notice the apple peelers are having a difficult time grating cheese. Although they sort of did the job, it was slow and cumbersome, and you could tell they didn't enjoy it much.

Walking over, you ask, "Can I help you grate the cheese?" Relief washes over their faces, and you try out this task.

You feel a surge of energy coursing through you as you feel the rush of being used for something purposeful, and you're actually good at it! You've affirmed that maybe you still have something to offer! But you still feel timid, wondering if this is really true.

Until you hear *His* voice over you...

"Daughter, I've created you for this unique purpose. Use it. Believe it. And help everyone and everything around you with this gift."

At first, you start small. You grate cheese in your home for your little people. It fills their bellies, and this brings you that sense of deep joy you haven't felt in a long time. The coolest part: it feels easy to you!

That's because you were created in this unique way.

A few months go by of using your unique purpose, and you get invited to a party. They want you to use your skills to grate all the cheese there! In fact, you suddenly notice that you even have an edge to slice cheese with, bringing your talents and gifts to use in a whole new way!

You attend this party and grate a wide variety of cheese delicacies you've never tried before. You're right next to the wine opener and apple peeler, and you notice how well you get along with them too!

There's a special harmony in this environment, and you love everything about it. People thank you for being there, because the party wouldn't be the same without you.

Without a second thought you say, "All glory to God because He created me this way to be used for His glory!"

They cheer this statement and praise God for the gift He's given you. In fact, you cheer for them as well because they made this beautiful event possible through the congregation of their gifts and talents. Each one is in line with their unique purpose, fulfilling God's plan in a harmonious and fulfilling way for Him and each one of them.

This is how it was meant to be. This is our aim, to be used with our unique purpose.

For a while, I didn't really know what my role or unique purpose was in church. At first, I tried being on the meal-planning team, but quickly realized there were others way more suited for that role than I was. I tried my hand at the greeting team, which seemed to fit with my extroverted personality but still wasn't quite right for me. It wasn't until I felt led to start teaching and discipling women one-on-one that I realized my unique gifts: speaking truth into others and cultivating a change of character through mentoring, writing, and coaching. Now I see myself being used in this way—at church, at home, through work—the way I've been created to be, feeling alive in my unique purpose as a participant in the body of Christ.

Have you been trying to be a cheese grater when you're meant to be an apple slicer? Have you been working in children's ministry only to feel more exhausted by this role and less fulfilled as you do it? Perhaps you're better suited to help plan for events, or maybe you're better off in the technology department creating videos or online materials for others. Maybe you were uniquely made to bring hospitality to others, be a prayer warrior for those hurting, or serve behind the scenes as you connect one-on-one with others. Maybe you're naturally suited to speak and preach, write books, develop curriculum, or serve on the outreach team. Maybe it flows into the real world, where you're a gifted teacher in public schools, bringing a much-needed light in the classroom. Or maybe you have natural management and leadership qualities that have helped you progress in your business, and you've been able to provide instruction and insight to others wanting to develop their own. Maybe you have a heart for children, and you've found yourself involved in fostering or adopting them into your home. These are the unique qualities, passions, and gifts He's given each of us, but it takes some exploring (try a few personality tests; here's a free one: https://www.16personalities.com/free-personality-test) and sometimes trial and error to discover them, as well as how it's all used together through the body of Christ. This is how you discover your unique purpose.

We each have an overarching purpose as God's daughters. We have been born with purpose, no matter what our gifts or talents are.

But where we come alive—where we feel fulfilled and what enables us to connect more with our Creator—is when we discover and use our unique purpose: the talents, spiritual gifts, and characteristics we've each been uniquely gifted with.

Although some of us may have similar gifts to add to

the table, we each have unique experiences and various passions—for a reason. We each play a distinct role in God's Kingdom—to be used for His glory. "Just as a body, though one, has many parts, but all its many parts form one body, so it is with Christ" (1 Cor. 12:12). And the way we are best used is by applying the unique gifts and unique genetic makeup He's given us to create things, help mobilize people, bring community together, love others, and cultivate something beautiful out of whatever you've been through.

There will be different seasons where your gifts come alive in new and different ways. Your purpose, or more specifically your unique purpose, can't be taken away from you. It will be used in one way for a specific role for one season and in another way for a different season.

Which brings me to my second question: what's your calling?

CALLING

I always thought calling was singular. One thing. And if you didn't know what that one thing was, you were doomed.

But there's a problem with this. Say you're "called" to be a dancer. That's your one calling in life. You've loved it since you were little, dancing around the room, twirling and performing pliés for your family at Christmastime. You've dreamed of performing onstage with the other performers someday. You push your body through grueling poses for thousands of hours, through expensive private college programs for performing arts, and hire pricey coaches to help you get there.

Then one day, you've made it! You are on the grand stage performing *The Nutcracker* in New York City! This is it. This is what you've been designed to do. This is your calling in life.

Then you get older. It gets harder to keep up. Other dancers become better. And eventually you are passed over.

This crushes you. You thought this was your calling in life! Now what are you supposed to do? The problem is that you believe your calling is singular.

I'm called to be a mom of three kids. I'm called to be a wife to my husband. I'm called to be a dental hygienist. I'm called to be an author and speaker. I'm called to foster kids. I'm called to Idaho. Each of these callings on my life can end. They are not my purpose, even though I use my unique purpose within each of these callings. But calling is the role that you play and that you are called to by the Caller for the season of life you're in.

What happens if my kids pass away unexpectedly? I'm no longer called to nurture their hearts anymore. What if my husband leaves me? What if my role as a dental hygienist doesn't fulfill me anymore? What if being an author and speaker is short-lived and so is fostering kids? What if we end up leaving Idaho?

Our calling can change. Our purpose cannot. God may call us for a season in a different role than we were doing before, but He will demonstrate to you what unique gifts and purpose you have to add to that role. You may love your calling for one season, but then find it's not what you feel passionate about anymore in a different season. Perhaps God called you for a season but is now inviting you to a different role you are meant to play.

There is also a problem when people connect their purpose to what they do. The role they've been given in life—say, a ballerina—seems to be their sole purpose in life. But this is false. When we place our purpose in our position, we risk wrecking our hearts when we lose that job, face being an empty-nester, ready ourselves for retirement. That position goes away and you think your purpose goes with it—because you think your purpose is in what you do, not in *who* you are.

This is why women fall apart when they subconsciously believe their purpose is in something that can shift. A college-age woman can feel purposeless as she transitions into the work world. A working forty-year-old woman can think she's failed her purpose because she's never married and never had kids (because society tells us this is what you're supposed to do to have value). A mom of three young kids struggles in her purpose because her life revolves around them and she's too tired to do anything else. When the kids are grown, she feels a sense of purpose-lessness because her identity was wrapped up in mother-hood, and she doesn't know who she is outside of this role she has played for twenty-five years. You retired from your career and now you don't know what your purpose is.

Our purpose cannot be in what we do. Roles change.

Our callings can change. You must not put your purpose in something that rusts or collects dust or shifts with the economics of society or based on the people you surround yourself with. To do so sets your heart up for failure. You must remember your purpose comes from the internal substance of Whose you really are.

God will invite you to explore all the ways you are gifted to be used for His glory. Sometimes you may find yourself on a stage or at a large party being used for God in what seems more significant ways. Other times, it will be for that one person in the private corner of your home. Both roles are significant. Neither is better than the other. This is the truth we must remember again and again so we don't become snared by pride, competition, or selfishness.

Don't run away from your calling when the Caller is telling you to use your gifts. Don't compare yourself to her when her gift or talent seems more special than yours.

Friend, don't be afraid to shine. But in the same way, don't be so focused on yourself that you forget the Creator who created you to shine through the talents He's given you. This is how you will deepen your sense of purpose. This is how you will fulfill your callings in life. This is how you will become saturated with deep satisfaction that overflows into all aspects of your life.

Do you have a hard time knowing your purpose? Ask yourself:

- What is it that I love?
- What comes naturally to me and is something I enjoy?

- How do I typically respond to others?
- Do I use words, actions, or some other way to communicate my ideas and feelings?
- Maybe I'm more of a thinker instead of a feeler?
- Maybe I love being active, or would rather spend time alone and in a quiet place?
- Maybe I'm good with numbers and organizing data?
- How do I experience true joy, elation almost indescribable, when I'm serving with my unique gifts, talents, and characteristics that He's given me?

After you ponder these questions about yourself, how can you use these internal gifts and characteristics in the various environments or ways God's called you to serve?

How can you use your specific gifts in motherhood, or singlehood, or widowhood?

How can you use your unique experiences while being on mission, serving those around you?

This is how you tap into your potential, your true identity, as you embrace your unique purpose and callings in life—completely changing the trajectory of your life.

This is the real Truth:

- You are wonderfully and beautifully made (Psalm 139:14).
- You may never be able to grasp how wide, how long, how high, and how deep His love is for you. But when you do grasp even a sliver of this love, it will fill you to a measure of fullness you will have never experienced before (Ephesians 3:18–19).

- You've been created to do good things in His name, not for your sake but for His to bring honor, glory, and praise to Him (Ephesians 2:10).

Your purpose is to bring honor and glory to God through your unique gifts, talents, and characteristics, and to fulfill that by embracing the various callings (roles) God calls you to.

And through your unique purpose and by accepting His callings, you will know who you really are. The more you pursue Him out of love for Him, the more you will know and desire what He wants for your life: "Delight yourself in the Lord, and He will give you the desires of your heart" (Psalm 37:4, ESV). You will get clarity in your direction and confidence as you move forward with all that God has in store for you. You will continue to discover more about yourself, the unique gifts you contain, and embrace the roles you've been invited to walk out. Not to do so—to reject His call and sit stagnant with your gifts—will stagnate your soul, leaving you feeling useless and discontented.

* * *

I was sitting in the nosebleed section with thousands of women in attendance.

This conference had all the motivational speakers, power-packed content, and an energy that sparked action. It was busy, alive, and brought powerful "aha" moments.

Yet it was in one of the quieter moments that my soul

was stirred—through a song sung by a woman whose voice graced me through the penetrating stillness of the crowd. Standing in awe, soul resonating, tears flowing, I soaked in God's presence through these words:

> You call me out upon the waters,
> The great unknown where feet may fail,
> And there I find You in the mystery,
> In oceans deep,
> My faith will stand.
> And I will call upon Your name,
> And keep my eyes above the waves,
> When oceans rise,
> My soul will rest in Your embrace,
> For I am Yours and You are mine.[1]

The words felt like they came from God Himself. Like Peter, God was calling me out upon the waters where feet may fail. "'Yes, come,' Jesus said. So Peter went over the side of the boat and walked on the water toward Jesus" (Matt. 14:29). Peter had faith. Faith in Jesus. Faith to act against all better judgment. Amid the storms and winds swirling around him, against all logic that gravity would defy him, he managed to get out of the boat.

What was the reward for his faith? He walked on water! Something impossible for any human to do (unless you have flotation devices on your feet).

Can you imagine what this must have felt like for Peter?

All the emotions, the energy, the adrenaline flowing

through him, a surging force of life stronger than he thought possible.

Yet when I read this story, I can't help but wonder where the motivation came from for Peter to even think of stepping out of the boat. When you read the story, it seemed like it was Peter who initiated the idea to get out of the boat, not Jesus. "'Lord, if it's you . . . tell me to come to you on the water'" (Matt. 14:28). Where did that idea come from; where did that desire emanate?

Five years ago, I was sitting content in my boat. It was a cozy boat, full of many comforts: material possessions, minimal judgment from others, quietly living my life the way I personally saw fit. I enjoyed the presence of Jesus in my life, but the idea of stepping out of my boat was the furthest thing from my mind.

Content as I was, something was lacking. A subtle ache in my heart refused to be satisfied with life aboard my little boat. I sought to fill that ache with things I thought would fill it: friendships, possessions, achievements. They would satisfy for a season, but the ache would always return, and with it the subtle discontent with life aboard my little boat.

It was through that subtle discontent I began to understand Peter's motivation for getting out of the boat. Jesus's presence upon the raging waters outside his little boat ignited his deepest passions, turning them from a subtle voice of discontent into a driving passion that could not be ignored. After that, life aboard the ship was simply not a palatable option any longer.

The more I began to seek God in the stillness of my day, the more I felt Him prodding me, poking me, churning the dormant desires in my soul, making life aboard my ship less and less attractive.

You see, my boat was keeping me from living a life of soul-filling abundance, more than I realized. Only by obediently stepping out in faith, by God's prompting, was I able to discover what it feels like now to completely follow Jesus in ways that wholly satisfy.

Paul Sohn, in *Quarter-Life Calling*, describes it like this: "When it becomes God-directed instead of self-directed, our life suddenly takes on a true sense of meaning and purpose."[2]

My boat was keeping me from experiencing God. When I got out of it, I experienced greater satisfaction than what I was experiencing at a distance from Him before.

Is God inviting you to get out of your boat to revive your heart and release your purpose?

Think about it: have you ever been struck by a song, beautiful scenery, or words on a page that speak to you in that moment of time, communicating deeply, capturing your heart, bringing up deep desires from the forgotten places of your soul? You soul comes alive with that surge of emotion, brings awareness to that ache, filling your soul in ways difficult to describe or understand, but you just know that you can't stay still any longer.

Those moments are not simple coincidences. The Lover of your soul is calling you to take inventory of your life, make a change, take a deep breath, and step out onto the waters!

The current richness I feel in my soul is palpable. A fuller life. A life that makes my heart soar. A life without limits following His presence. A life in which I'm expressing my unique purpose and fulfilling the callings the Caller has invited me into with Him.

Actions led by faith in the One who guides my steps fill me with a deeper sense of purpose because of my obedient devotion to Jesus. Genuine trust in God has become a whole new way of living. It is exhilarating at times, like the feeling I'm sure Peter felt when he became the first ever water-walker.

The thing about water-walking, though, is that God doesn't guarantee it will be free of trials. He doesn't guarantee that it will always be comfortable where He beckons you to follow. He doesn't even guarantee that you will be successful. However, He does guarantee that He will always be right there with you, and catch you if you sink: "But when he saw the strong wind and the waves, he was terrified and began to sink. 'Save me, Lord!' he shouted. Jesus immediately reached out and grabbed him" (Matt. 14:30–31).

Some days I begin to sink in the waves of stress, doubt, and worry. Some days, overwhelming demands threaten to pull me under the watery abyss. Some days I take my focus away from the One who can calm the storms around me. Moments of fear and failure seek to consume me and lead me back to my hiding place—back to the comfort of my boat.

But I press on because I know that Jesus is with me. I

trust that He will catch me when my focus wanes and my feet begin to fail. I press on because I know that life aboard my boat will never compare with life upon the water.

John Ortberg says, "There is danger in getting out of the boat. But there is danger in staying in it as well. If you live in the boat—whatever your boat happens to be—you will eventually die of boredom and stagnation. Everything is risky."[3] Success will always be, simply, taking the first step to get out of the boat—even if things don't go as planned.

I would rather experience what it's like for a moment to "walk on water" with Jesus, to release my fears and be released for His purpose, even with the possibility of wavering or sinking in the waves. Because where feet may fail, Jesus will not.

Borrow This Releasing Prayer
When Words Are Few

Heavenly Father, I sense You inviting me into something with You. But I'm afraid. I'm afraid I will fail. I'm afraid of rejection. I'm afraid to put myself out there when there are so many unknowns. I don't want to write off all those things as coincidences. I want to believe that You are beckoning me to something more with You. Help me have the courage and desire to step out of the safety of my boat and walk on water with You. In Jesus's name, amen.

CHAPTER 13

Water-Walking

"Are you up for talking about something crazy?" my husband said from the end of the bed where he was perched.

I was lying on the bed half asleep. It was only eight-thirty p.m., but it felt like midnight after a long day of taming three toddler tornados. Normally talking crazy is totally my thing. But tonight, I just wanted to conk out and wake to new mercies in the morning.

I mustered something like, "Mmmm, yeah, sure" as I propped myself up on my elbow, looking at him sleepily.

He seems a bit wary. I wonder what's up with him.

His tone showed signs of apprehension. "So..." He shifted uncomfortably. "You know how Tim and Julie are in the process of buying a ranch. And you know how we found out they lost funding at the eleventh hour and they were given an extension to find enough funds to make this happen. And you know how they need a miracle to move this mountain forward. Well..." He hesitated. "I called him and asked to be specific on what funds they really need..."

I knew where this conversation was heading. Alarm bells sounded off inside me. He continued to share with me the exact amount our new friends needed to make this purchase of a sixty-acre ranch in southern Idaho, a ranch they felt called to turn into a Christian retreat, event, and wedding center.

Everything in me screamed, *NO! This is too risky! This isn't smart! We hardly even know them! Yes, we have this amount, but it will wipe out all our savings we've worked so hard for, with just a tiny bit left over to live.*

He saw me tense up but kept going. "Rachel, I keep praying about this...and I keep sensing God is telling me that we are the ones to make this happen. We have just the right amount of funds to do this. I can't help but think maybe this is what God has been preparing us to do."

Shaking my head in panic, I declared, "Noooo... absolutely not. Jeff, we can't do this! You're quitting your job! We just bought an RV and we've been planning on using those funds to keep us afloat as we travel around the country. We need it to live! We need this money too!"

"I know. I get it. But," he went on, "what if we aren't supposed to travel in the RV? What if the RV was meant for us to live in on this ranch for a while? We were going to stay there for the month of October anyway. Plus, the idea of homeschooling our kids while being on the road is getting less and less appealing, if you know what I mean." He half joked, but in all seriousness, he was right about that.

"I keep praying for God to intervene, to send someone else to fill their need," he continued. "And, well, I keep sensing that we are the ones to do it. The amount they need is coincidentally what we have with just a little bit left over to keep us afloat until our house closes. Once our house is sold, we should have enough funds again to cover us for a while longer until we figure things out."

Until we figure things out. It *was* crazy talk.

Wrapping my mind around another new shift to our current faith-driven journey, I sat there processing it all at lightning speed. I knew Tim and Julie needed the funding by the next day; otherwise they would lose the ranch. There was a sense of urgency to this, and if we were going to decide, we had to do it fast.

The decision my husband had made to quit his job a few months prior in May 2018 opened a plethora of doors we never knew were there before. Along with the decision to quit his job, we were given the option to sell or rent our home, because there was no way we could afford to live in the pricey hills of Southern California without his income. Although my income was growing, it wasn't cutting it yet. Our savings would dwindle ever so quickly by staying where we were. Ironically, we had already been talking about moving away from city life—traffic and the "keeping up with the Joneses" pressure. I adored my home, but it wasn't worth it anymore. My husband was miserable in his job—fighting bouts of depression and burnout. Perhaps

God was calling us out of the American dream into a God-driven dream?

So in July 2018 we decided to put our house up on the market to sell. But the next question was, "Where are we going?" We literally had no idea.

God, I need you to direct us. The timing feels right. Where do you want us to go?

The country didn't always appeal to me. Most of my life I'd been more excited about the city. Growing up in the small mountain town of Paradise, California, there was nothing to do except to go to the one local theater with smashed-down seats or hike down to the flume. I was ready for the glitter and glam of the city.

We married in 2006 and followed career paths leading to the suburbs of Los Angeles—a sprawling city of millions—but never anticipated being here long-term. However, months turned into years and years turned into a decade later. Moving to the country seemed out of the question, since we both enjoyed the status of our salaries. So we did the next best thing: we moved to a wannabe-country town outside of LA County, which provided more respite for our souls. It was good, for a season. But as I've come to learn, what was good for one season may not be good for the next season.

Let me give you that permission right now: you have permission to make shifts in your life. You have more options at your disposal right now than you think. Don't be afraid to seek God with your wild, outlandish dreams and ask Him to infuse you with His (which may line up more fully than you believed possible). It's time to live a life on purpose, taking risks even if other people don't fully understand.

You can release responsibility for some things that feel soul-sucking in your life to make room in your heart for those that are more life-giving. You can let go of the guilt of thinking you have to do things only one way. You'll soon discover there are multiple ways. Not one way is better than another. You can free yourself from the guilt that you're a bad daughter for moving away from your parents, because the financial toll it's taking on you to live in an expensive area and work in a job you hate (but pays well) isn't worth it anymore. Or you can free yourself from the guilt that you're a bad mom for pursuing your dreams and run wild after what God has put on your heart. Because guess what? This will spark a passionate, revitalizing fire in your heart, which will positively affect every other aspect of your life.

You don't have to explain your life to anyone. Just make the shift you know you need to make. If your season calls for a scarf and boots instead of tank tops and shorts, do it, even if everyone else around you is wearing tank tops and shorts. You do you. You do what God's called you to do.

We certainly did. My husband left his successful job, I retired from my well-loved career as a dental hygienist that I had worked so hard for, we left a church we initially loved, and I gave up coffee. Sadly, I had to switch to chai lattes due to intestinal issues from that beloved black bean. Suffice it to say, what was good for a season wasn't good for this season anymore.

This was us in this season. We no longer felt like we were supposed to stay where we were. But we had no idea where to go.

That's when the RV idea came up.

Jeff basically grew up living in an RV. His parents have always had one to camp in, and that's how they would spend their vacations. It's still an important thing in his family. Because of this, we've rented RVs and enjoyed the benefits of camping "in style" while hanging out with his family. Honestly, this girl doesn't mind having a toilet, shower, and fridge while camping instead of a thin tent, camp food, and sleeping on the dirt in sleeping bags.

We thought about buying an RV *someday*. Someday suddenly presented itself. The next step on this adventure with God. So, we purchased a forty-one-foot fifth-wheel in June 2018, preparing ourselves for full-time living on the road. To be honest, I had *no idea* how *huge* a forty-one-foot RV was. And maybe God didn't specifically tell us to buy *this* RV (I may be a bit compulsive). I simply thought, *If we're going to be living in this thing, it needs to be* big *to fit our needs!* The day we brought home this RV (which I found a super good deal on, by the way) was the day I wondered if we had made a giant mistake.

In the beginning, we planned on being on the road for a year, which made sense for this type of RV. But soon the timing dwindled to six months, then to four as we thought about the complexities of the situation. When Jeff approached me about the ranch, we had already narrowed it to three months max.

As we prayerfully asked the Spirit to lead us on this journey, things continued to shift. We really had no idea what we were doing, except prayerfully making decisions we felt were confirmed by the Holy Spirit. When we both felt that deeper, inner peace, we went for it. It was exhilarating living completely dependent on His leading.

What if we all lived in this way? Obediently following wherever His Spirit leads us?

All throughout God's Scripture, God speaks. He speaks to Moses, leading him and His people out of Egypt, a place of bondage, to the promised land He planned for them. He speaks to Esther, telling her to hold off speaking until just the right time to save her people from death. He speaks to Joseph through dreams, Gideon through fleece, and Balaam through something as odd as a donkey. He speaks through peace: "Let the peace of Christ rule in your hearts" (Col. 3:15, NIV). He speaks through thoughts: "[God] who forms the mountains, who creates the wind, and who reveals his thoughts to mankind" (Amos 4:13). He speaks through the inspired Word of God: "All Scripture is God-breathed and is useful for teaching, rebuking, correcting and training in righteousness" (2 Tim. 3:16).

God speaks through you, other people, objects, sunrises and sunsets, and timely texts from a friend. You probably write these off as chance, but to do so, I think, sabotages your faith and denies the tangible presence of God in your life.

I sensed God calling us to Idaho, specifically the Boise area. Having written it off before as too cold (this

California girl likes her heat), suddenly I felt there was a distinct draw to this place. There were practical reasons for considering it—less expensive to live, family atmosphere, still close enough to visit family in California. After a bit of research, I discovered Boise is like the oasis of Idaho! Meaning I could just barely tolerate the winters there. Barely.

God knew.

There was a small town about thirty miles north of Boise that specifically caught my attention. There was nothing special about this town itself. A simple, quiet town with lots of farms nestled below a ring of hills and low mountains. When I heard the ranch our friends Tim and Julie were purchasing happened to be in the same location, I couldn't help but wonder if God was also inviting us to this place.

We decided to connect with them and hear more about their pursuits with their ranch. We tried countless times to connect. Finally, after another almost failed attempt, we made a quick change of plans, meeting at a local McDonald's with a play area so our kids could run wild as we talked. We absorbed in two hours as much interrupted conversation as we could about their vision for this ranch and their story of what God was calling them to do.

I was awestruck.

So much excitement, admiration, and wonder came forth from that conversation. Buried dreams broke the surface of my mind and my husband's too and mingled with theirs. A crazy vision we had for something beyond what we could have ever imagined made its way into the forefront of our

minds as we heard Tim and Julie reveal the passion and purpose behind this place. When I heard Julie say, "Our vision
and goal for this place is to have people come and be *refined
and restored* by God..." my husband and I looked at each
other and laughed. They had no idea what they had just said
and how God was using this for confirmation.

Refine and Restore. She had no idea about my ministry
name. No idea I was writing a book with that title. No
idea that those words meant so much to me. It was another
confirmation of many confirmations God was demonstrating to us, leading us toward this place. We weren't even
sure what this confirmation meant except to stay connected
with them. Stay near. Stay close. More would be revealed
in time.

I had no idea God would require so much of us to follow
this invitation by Him.

Sitting upright now on the squishy bed—two weeks before moving into our RV, a week before Jeff would officially
be without a paycheck, and one day to decide on a huge
financial risk toward a dream we didn't even know we
wanted—Jeff looked at my face for clues. But the human
part of me overrode any sort of Spirit intuition in me.

"I can't do this... I can't decide this. We have to kneel,
right now. We have to give this up to prayer and let God
speak. If it's meant to be, He will make it clear."

So we took the throw pillows off our bed (the ones my
husband thinks are pointless) and laid them on the floor for
our knees. With our eyes closed, we laid our request before
God.

What happened next was nothing short of amazing. With fear and panic sweeping over my body from our conversation, within one minute of praying, total peace and calm washed it all away so powerfully I could have fallen asleep. Warmth flooded my heart. Longing was suddenly birthed for this ranch. It made no sense, and yet it made perfect sense.

As Jeff continued praying, I heard myself say out loud, "Yes, yep, it's us. It's us. We need to call them. It's us." Tears of joyful submission fell down my cheeks as I acknowledged and accepted this holy invitation.

Within minutes, we called our recent friends and new business partners with the good news: we would provide the necessary funds for them to close the deal on the ranch.

Here we were on a new path and plan, one we never saw coming and yet felt completely sure of God's leading. It was both daunting and electrifying to realize our lives would never be the same again.

Within weeks, our home was sold, and we moved from the bustling sprawl of Southern California to the rural hills of southern Idaho, never having visited ahead of time. But we trusted in His leading, a leading that whispered to my anxiety-ridden heart, *You will figure it out when you get there.*

The "figure it out when you get there" was indeed that. We arrived at the ranch at four-thirty p.m. one afternoon with our three very wound-up children after a ten-hour drive. I was antsy to get our RV set up. The RV had been sitting on the ranch for a month due to unforeseen events. We'd stocked it with food and connected power to the RV fridge so that it would be ready when we arrived. Once we arrived, however, Jeff approached me with wide eyes after checking the RV and said, "It's going to be okay; don't freak out..."

My insides coiled. *What now?*

"So...we cannot sleep in the RV tonight. The fridge got ajar somehow, and everything is spoiled. The stench in the place is foul, babe. It's bad. *But* Tim and Julie said we can move into the manufactured home next to them with the kids. It will be fine. It has two bedrooms and it will work for now. In fact, I think it will be an even better setup than the RV," he said, trying to encourage me.

"You're kidding!" I said shrilly. "I want to be in the RV, babe. I don't want to live in that home. Did you see the inside of it? It's pretty gross!"

* * *

If this wasn't enough to blow my chill gasket, I found out the ranch still had no internet and no cell service that my husband promised would be available. Having a business that is solely online, with multiple coaching calls and a podcast episode I was recording with a high-profile person in five days, my chill tank cracked. I sucked in air, forcing my lungs to pull in enough to overcome the overwhelming feeling rising in my chest. I could feel my insides shaking—the buildup of so many fears, unknowns, and the discomfort of it all. This was the tip of the anxiety iceberg, or what I call an anxiety-berg—hundreds of other stress-filled things packed one on top of the other. This was the tipping point.

I need you to know something right now. I need you to know that trusting Jesus doesn't mean you will be free from fear. It doesn't mean you won't face struggles—mentally, physically, emotionally, or spiritually. It doesn't mean everything will work out according to your plans.

Trusting Jesus means you will experience fear, but He will provide a way out from it. You will face opposition, struggles, and blockades from the path you're on because of the enemy who wants nothing more than to remove you from the path and plan God has for you. You will think God's plan is one way, only to be redirected another way. But a redirection doesn't necessarily mean a wrong direction. He may take you on a path that's backward, diagonal, on backcountry roads that don't seem to be leading where you want to go. But He sees the full picture. He sees the best way through. We must trust He has a good path and plan in store for us, despite the detours and dead ends we face.

Our first night in our unexpected new home produced an unexpected attack to my soul. At four-thirty in the morning, my brain woke to feeling like I had ingested thirty cups of coffee while being on steroids. Okay, thirty cups of chai latte, since I had given up coffee a year before.

Neurons fired at light speed. I couldn't tame them. I breathed deeply, but peace wouldn't come. I spoke Scripture over my mind, fighting for His truth to win my mind back to His, but it wouldn't stop. Panic, stress, fear.

They forced their way in more forcefully than I'd ever experienced before.

I stumbled out of the bedroom into the living room, my world spinning out of control. To my right, the brown leather armchair perched on the teal carpet called my name. Wave after wave of panic crashed into me. The heavy breathing, mind swirling, and full-body shaking told me the truth: I was having a panic attack.

I curled up in the chair and bawled. I couldn't stop it. It was terrifying. Jeff woke, since the walls to the place are as thin as cardboard. Seeing the severity of the situation but unsure of how to approach me, he asked, "Are you okay?"

"Don't touch me," I shot back. "I...I think I'm having a panic attack. I just need space to breathe..."

He crept back into the moonlit glow of the room, eventually sitting with his back against the wall, head bowed in what looked like prayer. Likely praying over me.

I willed my mind to believe God would overcome this. I willed my thoughts to slow, and continued to breathe huge, gulping breaths into my airtight lungs. What felt like hours was maybe ten minutes as my heart began to slowly steady its beat. Shuddering breaths began soothing me, until my tears ceased. The flash frames of hundreds of images that raced through my mind began to slow down and still. I started to see my surroundings again. Finally I was calm. I sat there quietly, letting my mind still for several minutes before I turned to Jeff sitting a few feet from me to let him know I was okay again. I went back to bed, not wanting to discuss what just happened but knowing there would be a conversation about it later.

We found a quiet moment later that day, sitting on the old wood-beaten porch overlooking the new sight of endless golden hills before us. Processing through my panic attack and through the buildup of fears that had led to my demise, Jeff helped me identify each fear and see the options we had to alleviate the issues before us. It was a tender moment between my husband and me, a beautiful moment I wish didn't have to come from my experiencing something so terrible.

But isn't that often how God works? Bringing purpose in our pain, beauty from ashes, and light out of darkness? Would we appreciate restored grace if we never needed it in the first place? Would we ever need God if we were forever strong and never weak?

"My grace is sufficient for you, for my power is made perfect in weakness" (2 Cor. 12:9) is true all the time.

I believed in this ranch with my whole heart. I still do. I believed in the vision for this place as I walked the weedy, overgrown paths covered with goat heads (a nasty thorn new to me). I put my hands on the worn-down russet fences and rickety, aged buildings, seeing the potential that lay here. I visualized the people—men and women—who would become refined and restored here. It would be a much-needed place in this needy community and in the world.

But I didn't see us living here on the ranch. At least not right now. Not when so much work needed to be done and so many objects were prime for my kids to strangle or mangle themselves with. Not with the noise of the pack rats ripping at the insulation underneath waking me each night. Not as we transitioned from city living to full-blown boondock living. I needed an in-between. I also needed strong internet for my work, which was now our main source of income. To keep my anxiety at bay, I needed a place nearby to call my own where we could still steward the growth of the ranch but would provide a less cumbersome living arrangement, since we were here to stay.

Jeff agreed. He even agreed when I mentioned wanting to consider taking a low dose of anti-depression and anti-anxiety medication for this present stressful season.

In my pride, I never wanted to seek help in the form of a little pill. But new seasons call for new perspectives and new help. And to do the work God was calling me to do in this season, I knew this was the right next step.

Over the years, I've battled this anxiety battle, fighting it with counselors, meditation, deep breathing, stress-relief coloring, walking, singing, listening to worship music, praying, reciting God's Word over and over in my heart and mind...then repeating all of the above over and over again.

It's all helped. Believe me. There were seasons I was completely free from it. But sometimes a new season calls for new intervention. And this time I felt the peace of God saying, "It's okay; you aren't loved any less if you take medication for your struggle."

Following Jesus doesn't mean you will be free from panic attacks or anxiety. It doesn't mean you will be healed, although that can happen. It doesn't mean that things will be easier for you. Following Jesus means being stripped of your character—refined—and re-created into a Christlike image of Him—restored. It means having fear and peace at the same time. Pain and freedom. Joy and sorrow. It means, as Stasi Eldredge puts it, having defiant joy where "we can have joy in the midst of the lamentations of our lives."[1] He may call you into the fear-laden wilderness to help refine and strip away the parts of your character that need stripping, all for the sole purpose of restoring your heart and mind back to your need for Him and His truths.

I've never felt needier of Jesus than in this season of stripping. There are days I want to curl up into a ball and run away from the weight of it all. But God gently whispers, "You think you are meant to carry it all, but you're not."

I was reading in the book of John one day when this truth became clearer (John 6:1–15). There was a crowd of five thousand people following Jesus. It was becoming common. Jesus was performing miracles, defying church leaders, explaining a new covenant of truth, and healing the helpless. He was doing the impossible and the unthinkable. And with all the exciting things He was saying and doing, these crowds would forget they were following Jesus outside the city walls without bringing anything with them to eat. *Hangry, anyone?*

Noticing the hunger problem, Jesus asked one of the disciples, "Where are we to buy bread, so that these people may eat?" Jesus already knew what He would do, but He wanted to test the disciples to see what they would do. I imagine Jesus thinking, *Will they believe I can perform this miracle I'm about to do after all the other miracles they've experienced from Me?*

Another disciple spoke up: "Here is a boy with five small barley loaves and two small fish, but how far will they go among so many?" They doubted.

That's when Jesus commanded everyone to sit down and demonstrated a powerful truth among the many. It's a truth you may have missed too.

Jesus blessed the fish and loaves and began passing them in baskets among the crowd, asking them to eat until they were full. I'm sure some of them thought, *There's no way this will work, Jesus. I know you're pretty amazing and all, but we are talking about feeding five thousand people with a few puny fish and loaves. This is impossible.*

And yet the impossible was made possible, but not without their seemingly pointless action.

You see, Jesus wanted them to take a small step of action, providing the initial fish and five loaves. He wanted them to play a part, a key role, in fact, to allow the impossible to take place. He took what they offered and did the rest. They did what they could, and Jesus did what they couldn't.

We are not meant to feed the multitude by ourselves. We are not meant to create the miracle. We are not meant to carry the weight of the world upon our shoulders. We are meant only to do the little bit we are meant to do and trust God to provide the rest.

You are not meant to shoulder the entire burden of your spiritually lost children.

You are not fully responsible for whether your business succeeds or fails.

You need to stop saying yes to everything, only to become overwhelmed by doing *too much* for God, forgetting that He wants to show you how it can be done without causing burnout.

You need to stop saying no to everything because you see the impossibilities of it and don't trust God to take over.

You need to release control and allow Him to release you into this world to be used for His purpose, even if it seems small, or impossible, or insignificant at best.

Take that risk. Do what you can. Then let God do what you can't.

Friend, just take care of the two fish and five loaves—let Him do the rest.

Borrow This Releasing Prayer When Words Are Few

Father in Heaven, I know I can't do this on my own. But I also know I am not meant to create the miracle. I will start small, and do what I can with the little bit I know how. I will start pursuing the God-given dream You've put in my heart so long ago, and bit by bit move toward this desire. It won't be easy. At times I'm going to want to give up. But I choose to believe that You have a path and plan in this for me that will be worth the sacrifice, whatever that may be. Thank You in advance for what You've invited me to do with You. Help me steward this well. In Jesus's name, amen.

CHAPTER 14

Is It Worth the Risk?

I looked out at the sea of empty chairs. Okay, not quite empty; five brave souls filled five of the eighty lined up in rows.

I glanced at my team members, who doubled the number of people in the room. One manned the forty-plus books still lying on tables in the back. One worked the sound booth, readying the projection of my mic. One was at the door, ready to greet the minimum of forty who were supposed to arrive. The other two prepared for their roles to be group leaders and walk women through the material I had created. I stood onstage, checking the clock, praying people were simply delayed and more were coming.

But no more came.

Fifteen minutes after showtime, I shuffled my word-filled pages on the stand and willed my mind to go on. It screamed, *You're an embarrassment! Nobody cares about this! What a failure you are . . .*

Inside I was a scared doe wanting to run. On the outside, I stood bravely, forcing away any hints of my internal crumbling, and spoke my message of conviction to the five curious souls. I gave it my all, willing my head to believe there were hundreds listening. Yet the message pounded at me internally—God doesn't care about this, God didn't show up for you, God isn't trustworthy anymore.

After I spoke, we all came together in one small group instead of breaking off into five groups as I had anticipated. We shared stories, worked through the new insights discussed, and they promised to come back the following week for the next lesson.

After those five strangers left, I gathered my things and closed up the auditorium with my team. I still remember Molly saying, "You spoke with such authority, it sounded like you were preaching to a thousand women!"

I finally broke. Chin trembling, I cried and apologized that I had overestimated the number of women who would attend.

"It's okay!" she assured me. I wasn't so sure.

Driving home, I was a flood of tears. I wasn't just sad, I was sad-mad, as Joy and Sadness in the movie *Inside Out* would explain.

God, why did You tell me to do this, only to have five people show up? This is stupid! I wasted so much time away from my family preparing, spent money purchasing books, lost hours of sleep creating this material, only to have just five women show. Why, God?

There were streams of lights, thousands of cars filled with people rushing past my window as I sped in pain down the busy freeway toward home. So many people. So many souls to reach.

So many could have come. I wanted a crowd. I wanted to make a big impact. But I also wanted to shine.

Through the whizz of lights, a voice spoke powerfully deep in my heart: *How will you steward the many if you aren't willing to steward the few?*

I hated this response. My pride wouldn't allow it.

A few minutes passed, and I felt humbling conviction. His Spirit penetrated my heart, softening me. Tears of genuine sorrow now welled up as I saw the truth of my ultimate failure: pride.

Just because you take the invocation to walk on water with Jesus doesn't mean it's going to turn out the way you think it will. Taking the invitation to walk on water with Jesus, somewhere along the way I started to sink with my own self-focused glory. I wanted to experience the thrill of making an impact on many, but wasn't ready to say, "But if not, a few is okay too."

Deep down, my heart really did want to help others with the message God gave me. My soul enjoyed being used by God in the ways of speaking, writing, and mentoring. My mind said I wouldn't be disappointed if only a few showed up. But when reality hit, and my worst fear showed up in the open seats that night, it broke the pride I didn't realize was still there. In the embarrassment and pain of it, I was ready to throw in the towel and forget it had ever happened.

But God...

He challenged me to remember how He served the few. He reminded me of His tough love—allowing this to happen, so I might experience a refine-and-restore moment with Him that would cultivate my character in ways I couldn't see before. Would I have the heart to continue with only a few souls to empower?

It took more prayer and conviction, but I showed up to the task He called me to for the next twelve weeks. I changed the location to a smaller room, bringing a more intimate feel to the group. I kept preaching the material and swallowed my pride. Was it hard? You bet. Was it worth it? Absolutely. Were those women's lives impacted? They all said, "Yes!" Even more important, my heart was forever changed by this refining moment.

I think we may have forgotten something when we read the story about Peter walking on water toward Jesus. At one point, Peter takes his eyes away from Jesus. He loses his focus and falters, starting to sink in the waves (Matt. 14:30).

In the same way, I started with my eyes on His glory but slowly turned my eyes to my own glory. I was sinking but didn't know it until I was fully submerged. Jesus extended His hand, asking if I was willing to still do this with Him, together. Standing up, week after week, for five women was extremely difficult. Embarrassment was strong. My heart was heavy. To leave my three kids under three years old with their dad night after night, facing spiritual attacks, shedding some of my most vulnerable moments with others, and talking about an extremely sensitive topic... There's no way I could have done that on my own.

Even now, as I write, speak, and mentor women through my coaching programs, I'm reminded of how much I need to keep my focus on God to do this job well. I can't overcome my pride without Him. It will sneak back in if I let it. I can't be a loving wife, intentional mom, connected friend, respected leader, and honorable daughter of the King unless I take His hand and stay focused on Him. I'm learning what Hannah Brencher wrote: "Living fully means giving up control and still being okay with the outcome."[1]

Accepting those water-walking invitations by God isn't going to be easy. They may be intimidating. Our focus tends to waver. The outcome may not be what you wanted it to be. But you will experience a side of God you wouldn't know otherwise. You will become refined by Him and restored by His love as you live out the impossible through Him.

Your water-walking experience may be:

- Inviting a new friend to church with you despite the possibility of ridicule.
- Starting a ministry with the risk of failure in your path.
- Writing that book even though you don't know how to start.
- Connecting with your children when you'd rather check out.
- Loving your husband when you don't feel loved back.
- Paying for someone's rent when you can hardly afford your own.

As I've continued to walk out my calling in ministry, I've seen how God has used the painful experiences I've faced to help refine my character and restore my identity to reflect more closely His. Embracing these refine-and-restore moments is important—it has encouraged spiritual growth due to the challenges and struggles I've faced instead of my choosing the complacent life that is easy and mundane. I'm surrendering instead of controlling. Serving instead of sitting. Believing instead of retreating. This is the truth. Claim it. And live it, because to not do so is like leaving your car on, running idle in the driveway, and forgetting what its purpose is.

BUT IF NOT

A banquet of uneaten sushi platters lay tantalizing before us on the chipped granite counter atop our island. I looked at the clock: 12:03 a.m.

I tapped my phone again, but there were no messages. No texts. No missed calls.

Glancing at my husband, I could see the extreme confusion with flashes of fury in his eyes. He looked how I felt.

This was supposed to happen. God…why aren't you pulling through?

Two years of navigating this path and plan barreled through my mind, every Spirit-led moment leading to this planned moment, or so I thought. We believed the verse: "Faith is being sure of what we hope for. It is being certain of what we do not see" (Hebrews 11:1, NIrV).

We were sure of what we hoped for. We felt certain of what we could not see. Because we had faith God was leading us, God would come through on a promise He had for us, and so we continued walking this out in the ways we felt Him leading. However, we expected Him to lead us to a happy ending.

In the aftermath of free-falling faith, the parachute seemed to have ripped, leaving us crashing to our deaths. My spirit was crushed. I wasn't so sure about God anymore. The foundation of my faith splintered. The war within myself about what I knew and believed about God brought me to a crisis of faith as I asked the question:

Did I make this all up? But, that's impossible! So many signs! We fasted for three days! We were faithful! Why, God, would you ask us to leap, only to let us shatter into pieces on the ground?

At 12:16 a.m. we succumbed to the reality. She wasn't coming, our foster daughter we had prayed for and believed would come on a certain date and time. That date, June 18, 2016, wasn't going to be the day for our family to grow.

The rumbling in my belly became too much. The celebration with sushi died when midnight hit. There was no call, no sign of this faith-filled adventure becoming a reality.

I shoved down the raw fish dipped in wasabi-mixed soy sauce, feeling the burn as it filled my hungry belly. Although it satisfied the body, it dissatisfied the soul. What was meant to be a celebration felt like a permanent cremation as we buried our wild foster-adoption journey into the ground.

Can I be clear? I never wanted to take this journey in the first place. Fostering, let alone adoption, was never on my radar. With three kids still in diapers beckoning for their every need, I was far from excited to bring in another one to care for. And looking for a girl with the same birthdate as my daughter—making it her "twin sister"—felt completely nuts.

But it was the story we were led to and a story I'm still trying to make sense of.

This story isn't comfortable to share. I struggle even sharing it now with you, because I'm accepting a wide range of assumptions. We've already received a host of mixed responses in the wake of this failed faith journey.

Many close friends knew our story as well. They walked through it with us, prayed with us, gave us the faith to keep going. But when the date passed without the arrival of a girl to celebrate, it left us grieving, deeply embarrassed, and at a loss for words.

We won't ever know in totality how God works or how the Holy Spirit works, but it doesn't mean God isn't real and that the Holy Spirit didn't speak. It doesn't mean God left you and abandoned you, even though it feels that way. I've experienced this in my life. I've also seen it through multiple other people in the Bible.

Joseph was a young man who had a dream of ruling over his family—of them bowing down to him. I'm sure in his dream he saw himself in rich robes, delegating decisions, and enjoying the power he had. In what I believe was his own ignorance, he shared this with his brothers, who didn't share the same enthusiasm for his vision.

He felt like God had made this clear. He believed this would happen.

But then his journey took him on some major unexpected detours. Over the next twelve years he experienced being thrown in a pit to die by his brothers, sold as a slave, pursued by his master's mistress, whom he denied and yet he was framed and thrown in prison. He was likely chastised, beaten, ridiculed, and the furthest from being considered the king's right-hand man.

Yet God finally brought some truth to his story. Just not in the ways he likely anticipated.

Joseph was near to God, even through all the suffering. I wonder if he thought, "Wow, God gave me this vision and I expected to have reached that image by now. Did I make it up? Was God really speaking to me? Maybe I didn't understand Him correctly. I obviously didn't understand Him correctly about ruling over my family since I'm stuck in jail."

However, in jail he still became known for interpreting dreams and visions. I wonder how he was known for that when his original dream hadn't come to fruition yet. Perhaps there were other moments when God fulfilled the visions He received.

Eventually, Joseph interpreted a dream for the king, a dream that led to his release and put him on a pedestal next to the king, who valued his insights and ability to interpret what God shared. His dream finally came to fruition, but he had to go through trials, embarrassment, and multiple moments that didn't go as planned.

There's another man, named Job, who endured years of suffering and torture and yet believed God still loved him and had a good path and plan for him.

Shadrach, Meshach, and Abednego proclaimed they would not bow down to any other god than God Himself, even though it meant being thrown in a fiery furnace for their faith. They proclaimed, "Our God whom we serve is able to deliver us from the burning fiery furnace, and he will deliver us out of your hand O king. *But if not*, be it known to you, O king, that we will not serve your gods or worship the golden image that you have set up" (Daniel 3:17–18, AMP, emphasis added).

But. If. Not.

Three words filled with life-changing perspective.

When I went through my foster-adoption journey, reaching the pivotal point where I faced the fiery furnace testing my faith (and my husband's too), I failed to proclaim, "But if not, Lord... I will still trust you, still praise you, and still believe you have a purpose in this despite what I believe right now." Where I failed was failing to believe the "but if not..." in our story, which led to the near destruction of my faith.

But... God is so faithful.

On the seventh day of the aftermath of shattered faith in God, I was sitting in my backyard oasis in Southern California, writing ferociously in my journal. Writing off God, I was readying myself to pour into a new, irrelevant project to release my pain. I gave up believing His Voice, or what I thought was His Voice, was leading me through life. The Holy Spirit and my understanding of it were shattered and left me massively confused. It was like trying to repro-gram your computer from a PC to a Mac. Can you even do that? I'm pretty sure it would completely frazzle the system and corrupt the entire thing.

My spirit was corrupted—until a significant moment that could only be orchestrated by the Ultimate Orchestrator.

I looked down at my buzzing phone. A text came through: "Are you home?"

My retired nanny, turned friend, turned little sister I've never had, wanted to stop by. She felt like I needed to know something.

Yeah, I need to know if God still exists and if I'm a looney who made this whole thing up.

I hugged her at the door, and then we walked in and she sat at my island while I leaned against the sink. The fracturing of my heart was evident in the air around us as she cautiously told me what she had just experienced.

"So, I was at the doctor's office this morning and something interesting happened. Sitting in the waiting room, I overheard a conversation by two nurses in the hallway. It was a little odd, like God was telling me to pay attention to them."

I shifted, uncomfortable but intrigued with where she was going with this.

"One shared she was pregnant, and she had decided on a baby name. She shared with the nurse the meaning, but not the name itself. I didn't catch the actual name she shared, and you know I'm not super blunt to just get up and go ask, but I felt like I needed to. I felt like there was a reason."

I shifted again, curious about what this story had to do with me.

She proceeded, "So...you know how you told me a while back that God gave you a name for this foster girl you're looking for in the foster system? You never shared this name with anyone because you said God told you not to share?"

I remembered. At this point, I thought, *There's no way she knows. Besides, was that even real?*

My eyes showed curiosity, teeming with hints of disbelief in what she was about to share. She finally said, "Was the name...Eliana?"

Emotions rose up within me at the familiarity of that name. A name I'd held on to and didn't share with anyone out of obedience to what God had told me. Complete shock overcame me as I growled, "How did you know?!"

"Oh, my God, it's true!" she exclaimed. The surprise in her voice demonstrated mutual shock.

As we processed this all through tears, a spring in my heart opened again that day.

What are the odds? Is this really all true, God? Did I hear You but just don't understand where You're going with this story? Is there still a chance we might meet her someday on different terms and circumstances?

A piece of my faith in God was restored that day. The odds of it being coincidental don't satisfy me. It can't be. I know I can't exactly prove the truth of this story to you except to ask that you trust me. But the way I see it: He knew this shattering of faith would happen. He knew I would second-guess everything and get to a moment like that day where I was ready to give up on Him. Therefore, He provided the proof I needed when it mattered most to know that He is real.

He still speaks. And although I still don't fully understand why this had to happen the way it did, He is continuing to bring evidence of His purpose in it even though it didn't go as planned.

I know you have a story you're still questioning: "Why, God? I thought you were in this with me." We all have them.

Maybe you've been praying for healing over your daughter, had a vision of her healed, believed it, only to visit her grave three months later.

Maybe you believe God will save your marriage and you're ready to fight for it, only to see your partner walk out the next morning, and you are unable to convince him to come back into your life.

Maybe you had a vision for a ministry path, a confirmation about a book you felt called to write, or someone said, "You're going to have a baby," only to find yourself questioning the truth of what you experienced.

We've failed to come face-to-face with three words, "But if not..." and apply this truth over our lives when life doesn't make sense. Or when it leaves us heartbroken. Or births fiery anger in you as you lose your trust in Him.

* * *

But if not, will you believe that He is good despite what the future holds? But if not, will you still believe that He has a purpose and plan for you, even when it doesn't work out the way you thought it would? Will you believe in His love for you, even when love hurts because it requires a refining of your character? Will you trust that He is ultimately seeking to restore your heart back to His love, His truth, and His guiding hands for your life above all else?

I see this clearly written all over Scripture.

- "See what great love the Father has lavished on us, that we should be called children of God!" (1 John 3:1)
- "'For I know the plans I have for you,' declares the LORD, 'plans to prosper you and not to harm you, plans to give you hope and a future.'" (Jer. 29:11)
- "I have loved you with an everlasting love; I have drawn you with unfailing kindness." (Jer. 31:3)
- "All Scripture is God-breathed and is useful for teaching, rebuking, correcting and training in righteousness, so that [we] may be thoroughly equipped for every good work." (2 Tim. 3:16–17)
- "In their hearts humans plan their course, but the LORD establishes their steps." (Prov. 16:9)
- "Jesus answered, 'I am the way and the truth and the life. No one comes to the Father except through me.'" (John 14:6)
- "But when he, the Spirit of truth, comes, he will guide you into all the truth. He will not speak on his own; he

will speak only what he hears, and he will tell you what is yet to come." (John 16:13)

- "Taste and see that the LORD is good." (Psalm 34:8)
- "Sanctify them by the truth; your word is truth." (John 17:17)

At some point, we have to ask ourselves: Am I going to believe the Word of God is true even when I don't feel like it is? Will I believe God is good even when I don't see good in my life right now? Will I believe God is trustworthy when my marriage is strained, when my friend dies in a car accident, or when my business venture fails? Will I believe God loves me even when I don't feel His love?

Lauren Daigle, Christian worship artist, says it so well in her song "You Say":

You say I am loved when I can't feel a thing
You say I am strong when I think I am weak.

Look up this song and play it right now on your phone, computer, sound system at home, or wherever you listen to music. It's so relevant to this issue of feeling one way but our faith pulling us toward the truth.

Do you believe He loves you when you're a hot mess? Do you believe He loves you when in your weakness you react harshly and lie to others about it? Do you believe He loves you when you're too tired to pray or too overwhelmed to turn to Him? Do you believe He loves you even when you turn away from Him? Do you believe He still loves you when you admit your limitations and need help? Do you believe He is cheering for you when nobody else is? Do you believe He believes in you when nobody else will? Because He does, friend. He keeps fighting for you when everyone else has given up. This is the depth of His unconditional love. A love we often forget.

I'm in awe of the things He is doing through this unexpected journey of us leaving everything behind, everything that was comfortable and easy, propelling us on a journey into the wild wilderness with Him. Even through the panic, the overwhelm, the uncertainties, the bank account getting fearfully low when we transferred our life savings for a hope and a dream that hasn't come to fruition yet, I see glimpses of a greater vision than I could ever imagine. It leaves me in wonder and awe and in fervent prayer as I seek to be refined and restored so I can keep my heart revived as I release my unique purpose into this world. I would not trade following God for anything else, even through the "but if not..." moments with Him. Those moments of sorrow, surrender, and sickness unveiled truths to my heart that showed my character needed refining, and truths about God's character that needed restoring in my soul.

And this is the process we all must accept to revive our hearts and release our purpose—to refine or strip away the lies and subtle sin issues holding us back from deeper intimacy with God, and restore our hearts back to the truth of who God really is, enabling our true identity to be revealed. This refine-and-restore process is the growth cycle that continuously purifies your heart, renewing your mind back to His truth so you can live out your unique purpose and the calling(s) God is inviting you into with Him.

I'm nobody special. I don't have some sort of superhuman spirituality over you or another person. You can do this. God has incredible invitations for you too. They may feel terrifying at worst, or uncomfortable at best, but your skin will tingle with excited anticipation of being used by Him, and you will be in awe of His indescribable power as He leads you through Holy Spirit whispers toward incredible adventures with Him. Friend, it's time to accept His invitations to be released for His purpose.

Seeing the wonder of God is immensely satisfying when we step outside of what we can do and step into what only He can do. But so often, we sit back in fear. Like the disciples in the boat who watched Peter walk on water toward Jesus, you may be sitting back, watching others do amazing, awe-inspiring things with God because you fear what He is inviting you to do.

But, friend, you don't have to be brave. You just need to stay connected to the One who is.

Borrow This Releasing Prayer When Words Are Few

Almighty God, now's the time. Now's the time for me to get out of the safety of my boat. Now's the time to help me pursue what I was uniquely created to do. Help me discover these gifts and the woman You've created me to be. I want to believe in the callings You've called me to. I want to experience water-walking experiences with You. I want to be awed by your grace, love, and the power of You in my life, so others will take notice of You too. When you invite me to "Come, and follow Me...," I want to trust and accept this invitation. I want to remember, "but if not..." I will still trust and believe You have good things in store for me. I'm still scared, but I know there's a deeper peace that follows when I listen and obey. I would rather risk with You, Jesus, than sit back in complacency, missing all the good You have in store. Help me to step out of the boat today. In Jesus's name, amen.

ACKNOWLEDGMENTS

I'm still sitting here in awe that God would allow me to publish this book for you. I'm deeply thankful God has given me this invitation to share this message that has been burning inside me for the past four years. And so I must lead with my devotion and expression of thanks to Him, because without Him, I would have nothing important to say. Lord, You have my all. I'm nothing without You. Thank You for using me in this way. I pray it revives the hearts of all who read it.

Next is a word to my husband, Jeff. Babe, thank you so much for taking the kids on trips to see cousins, friends, family (anyone!) so I could write as many words as possible in peace. Thank you for cooking meals, picking up the house, and giving me space to fulfill this calling God has given me to write inspiration and encouragement to others through my stories. You will receive twice the number of crowns in heaven for your humble servant heart and quiet behind-the-scenes presence here. My heart feels like it's exploding right now with how much love I have for you. You took one for the team when the deadline for this book hit, and you know it. Thank you!

My children—Gavin, Rylan, and Aria. Someday you will probably wrestle with your faith and ask these same questions. My hope is that by reading this book from your mama, your hearts will be revived when they need reviving, your characters refined when they need refining, your identity restored when they need restoring, and you will have the faith in God to be released to do the work God has called you to do. I love you three so incredibly much!

Thank you to Jennifer Dukes Lee for championing this book and its message with your beautiful foreword. So incredibly thankful for you and our friendship.

To my agent, Cyle. Thank you for believing in me as a writer and pushing me to get this book out there. Can't wait to pitch many more projects with you! You're amazing.

To my FaithWords team, specifically Keren Baltzer: thank you! Thank you for believing in this message and polishing it up for clarity, impact, and accuracy. Thank you Leeanna for taking over in the middle of it. Thank you both for all the work you do and continue to do to for God's Kingdom. Thank you to everyone on the FaithWords team whose hands touched a piece of this heartfelt project. I'm forever grateful for your time, skills, and expertise.

To my writer friends, you know who you are. Thank you for continuing to cheer me on when I need it most. For the

Voxer messages, texts, DMs, emails, Zoom video meetings, and all the other crazy forms of technology that we have to communicate with each other these days. I love how God has made our paths intersect and how we can cheer one another on with our projects. Community over competition!

To my Aspiring Author clients: there's a reason you feel drawn to words. God has a plan to use you in this way. Do as I did: step out of the boat with God, growing into the writer you are meant to be.

To my very best girlfriends who continue to love me and believe in what God's called me to do—thank you for your unwavering friendship, even though we don't talk as often as I wish. You know who you are.

To my parents, sisters, and brother—I love you and hope you continue to seek the truth of God through the Bible and are touched by the testimony of faith I carry.

To my podcast listeners, thank you for believing in the importance of personal and spiritual growth. Every one of your downloads encourages me to keep talking about this topic of refining and restoring our hearts back to His.

To everyone who has shared about this book online, written reviews, gifted it to friends and family, donated copies to the local library, basically done anything and everything to get the word out about how this book has changed your life...thank you! It means the world to me every time you hashtag #refineandrestore with a pic of the book or with something that relates to this message.

To my readers who encourage me to keep writing and sharing, thank you! You keep me true to my word as I continue to practice what I preach. Because if I'm not living out the message of this book, what's the point of me even writing it? I pray that you will seek revival for your heart, that you'll allow God to refine your character and become a truer version of the person He desires you to be, that He would restore the truth of your identity as you begin to understand God's true identity, and that you would step out in faith to release your unique purpose, passions, and God-given dreams into this world for His glory.

NOTES

Chapter 3

1   Lysa Terkeurst, *The Best Yes: Making Wise Decisions in the Midst of Endless Demands* (Nashville, TN: Thomas Nelson, 2014), np.

Chapter 4

1   E. W. Rice, *Orientalisms in Bible Lands.* Watchtower Online Library. https://wol.jw.org/en/wol/d/r1/lp-e/101970048#h=3.

Chapter 7

1   Lysa TerKeurst, *Uninvited* (Nashville, Tenn.: Thomas Nelson, 2016), 119.

Chapter 8

1   Rachael Rettner, "Technology Use Before Bed Linked with Increased Stress." Live Science. May 29, 2013. http://www.livescience.com/34807-technology-before-bed-increases-stress.html.

Chapter 12

1   Joel Houston, Matt Crocker, Salomon Ligthelm, "Oceans (Where My Feet May Fail)" © 2013 Hillsong Music Publishing Australia (APRA).

2   Paul Sohn, *Quarter-Life Calling* (New York, N.Y.: FaithWords, 2017), 18.

3   John Ortberg, *If You Want to Walk on Water, You've Got to Get Out of the Boat* (Grand Rapids, Mich.: Zondervan, 2014), 20.

Chapter 13

1   Stasi Eldredge, *Defiant Joy* (Nashville, Tenn.: Thomas Nelson, 2018), 10.

Chapter 14

1   Hannah Brencher, *Come Matter Here* (Grand Rapids, Mich.: Zondervan, 2018), 169.

ABOUT THE AUTHOR

Velkyz Tovilla / In Your Image Photography

Rachel Swanson is a dental hygienist turned best-selling author, national speaker, podcaster, and accredited Christian life coach. She has a deep-rooted passion to refine away the lies holding women back and restore their hearts back to God's truth. Her personalized coaching programs include spiritual growth principles plus other mentoring tools to enable women to walk in alignment with their unique purpose and release their God-given dreams into the world.

She and her family of five recently took a leap of faith, moving from the bustling sprawl of southern California to the rural hills of southern Idaho, to rebuild a broken-down ranch into an events, wedding, and retreat center. Follow along on her adventures at rachelcswanson.com.